# CAN'T AFFORD TO **FAIL**

PETERGAY DUNKLEY-MULLINGS

# CONTENTS

*Dedicated to all my family and friends, for the love and support on this journey.*

# CHAPTER ONE

The air cools, the sky darkens, and the onset of night brings a familiar dread. It's at this time of the day when I know I'll be at my lowest, when I will feel so completely abandoned. The same questions haunt me over and over. Why is this happening to me? Why can't I be with my son? Why is it me who is in the wrong?

Gray clouds bunch above the nearby Park Mountain hills, and a stiff breeze shakes the trees, as if to admonish me to get moving. In a few moments the rain will start, and I must find shelter. To my chest I clutch a black plastic grocery bag that contains all my possessions, save for the jeans, t-shirt, and sneakers that I'm wearing.

Wind courses over the shallow rolling landscape and raises dust off the unpaved streets that crisscross the neighborhood. When people think of Jamaica they imagine only the beaches, but I'm miles inland, in the flat wooded landscape just south of Santa Cruz.

I head down Coke Street, away from the commercial strip and into the residential section. I don't dream of venturing into wealthy Dunkley Town because its residents would never take in a runaway girl like me, especially one who's had a child. Around me, the few people still outside scurry for cover. We rush past each other and no one gives me any more attention than they would a stray dog.

At the next corner I take a left to proceed up the lane. A Toyota sedan barrels toward me and barely misses. Jolting with panic, I jump aside and glare at the driver. He didn't even bother to honk. My presence doesn't register on his face, as if I'm invisible.

He rounds the corner and disappears north on Coke Street. Although I resent that he didn't acknowledge me, I'm glad he didn't stop. Strange men in cars bring only trouble to someone like me.

Continuing on my way, I pass a row of houses, their windows illuminated from within. I try not to glance inside as I walk past, but I can't help myself. I see the occupants, protected from the coming storm and oblivious to me. I see them busy with the trivial diversions of their lives: watching television, talking to each other, eating dinner. These concerns are so basic, so ordinary, but something that has been wrenched from me.

I had no choice but to run away as I could no longer fight off my father's sexual advances.

But at the moment I can't dwell on that bitterness, I first have to concentrate on finding shelter before the rain starts. I have to get through tonight and then I can worry about tomorrow.

At the end of the street I reach my destination, a collection of partially completed houses in various levels of construction. They stand empty, the workmen gone for the evening. I duck around the bushes growing between the houses and disappear—I hope—into the gathering darkness. If someone spots me I could be chased away, or worse, set upon by prowlers who won't hesitate to violate a teenage girl they find alone.

Up ahead I spot a bungalow, its windows covered by sheets of plywood. The air grows heavy and moist as if the clouds are about to split open and drench me. A crack of thunder zings my nerves, urging me to hustle.

Reaching the bungalow, I work my way through the barbed wire fencing and then step carefully around the building scraps littering the ground. The first drops of rain pockmark the dirt. I decide to enter through a corner window. After setting my plastic bag beside my feet, I draw the knife I keep for protection and slide it under the plywood nailed to the window frame. I lever the knife against the board but it remains firm.

The wind whips big drops of rain that spatter against my t-shirt. Desperately, I twist the knife harder because if I get wet, then my night will be that much more miserable. Clenching my teeth, I struggle to loosen the board.

Rain hits the wall and mists my face.

The board loosens just enough for me to work my fingers between the board and the window frame. I stow the knife and slide both hands under the plywood. Pressing one knee against the wall for leverage, I yank hard. I feel the strain in my arms and across my back. The nails start to give just as the rain gets heavier.

Water drips into my eyes and down my cheeks. I taste salt and chemicals, realize that my tears and styling gel are mixed with the rain.

The effort of pulling at the board and the despair welling inside me become almost unbearable. Why must I suffer so? I want to break down and cry.

But if I do, then what? I'll only be worse off than I am now. To survive I can only proceed from moment to moment.

I clench my teeth with renewed determination and pull harder. The board wrenches free so abruptly that I stagger backwards a couple of steps before regaining my balance. I don't have time to congratulate myself. Snatching my bag off the ground, I drop it through the open window. Next, I pick up the board, set it cross-wise in the window frame, leaving room for me to slide inside.

Awkwardly, I contort my body through the opening and search the floor with my toes. I hang onto the window frame to keep from spilling inside, to avoid making noise or hurting myself.

Easing through, I at last stand inside the house. I reposition the plywood over the window, raindrops splattering through the gaps. Certain that no one has seen me, I back away and scan the inside of the house as best I can in the murk. Sheets of rain drum across the roof.

I take stock of where I am in the house. I've entered into what is to be a bedroom. Electrical wires dangle from a hole in the ceiling. Off to one side, a doorway opens to an unfinished bathroom, pipes sticking out of the concrete to mark where the sink and toilet will be placed.

Carefully, just in case I'm not alone, I creep into the hall and peek into a front room and what must be the kitchen. I step around building scraps on the floor.

My stomach rumbles from hunger. My last meal was lunch, six hours ago, and it had cost the last of my money.

Scoping out the empty rooms I hope the workmen had left behind something to ease my appetite—perhaps a forgotten bag of half-eaten fast food. Next to a stack of tile, I find a small bag of potato chips, empty except for the broken remnants along the bottom that I collect in one hand and eat. It's not even a mouthful and not at all nourishing.

I pick up a tarp, whisk it clean of sawdust and drag it to the bedroom. While the tarp provides little in the way of comfort, the fact that I won't be sleeping on the bare floor lifts my spirit a little.

4

Some nights I've slept on the ground beneath trees, more feral cat than human being.

I spread the tarp along a wall farthest from the window in case the board falls and lets the rain in. Sitting on the tarp, I lean against the wall and slide out of my sneakers.

I take a breath and acknowledge that once again, I've survived another day. But the relief doesn't last, and my fears and doubts begin to accumulate. My damp t-shirt presses against my skin and brings an uncomfortable chill.

Digging through my plastic bag, I pull out my other t-shirt to swap it for the one I'm wearing. I ball the wet t-shirt inside the bag, which I intend to use as a pillow.

I use my comb to rake the rain out of my hair. I'm hoping the activity distracts me from the dark thoughts gathering in my mind, but it doesn't.

The desolate room shrinks around me, compressing the sadness. Now the real struggle begins. There is nowhere to run to escape the turmoil inside me.

This loneliness and abandonment are all that I have. I have no idea what tomorrow will bring other than more neglect. More failure. More scorn.

My stomach rumbles again. I'm so hungry it aches.

I think of my mother. Her house is less than fifteen minutes away, yet it might as well be in Kingston, on the other side of the island. No matter her financial situation, she always had a plate to share. I can see her spooning the night's meal into the bowls of my five siblings and setting aside an extra portion for me. All I have to do is show up.

But I can't.

My father has banished me, threatened to kill me if he sees my face. Even my mother is powerless against his wrath.

What have I done to deserve this? What was my offense?

Simply put, I bore a child out of wedlock. And my father—a man who can't stay sober long enough to hold onto a job and who schemes to fondle me every chance he gets—accused me of disgracing the family.

My son's father, Mark Stewart, is just as derelict. Mark occasionally visits my son, yet he brings nothing to help with his care. No diapers. No food. And of course, no money. Though Mark was complicit in my pregnancy, he can drop by my parents' house and not be bothered by an ounce of remorse or subjected to any kind of recrimination.

Tears sting my eyes, and I begin to sob, once again returning to my ritual of misery.

I next picture my son, now two years old. I see him at my mother's table, eagerly awaiting his supper before being tucked into a warm, safe bed.

And where am I?

I am here, hiding like a mouse. Branded as unworthy for what I've done, condemned for being a young woman in a land that regards them as disposable as trash.

My friends turned against me. My family—brothers, sisters, cousins—all revile me. My name is spoken in low tones as if it is a curse.

How long can I live like this? At what point will that meager thread of fortune that has kept me out of the hands of violent criminals, disease, and drugs finally break? This abyss that I'm in yawns beneath me, and I swallow the terror that I may yet land in a terrible splat against its distant, rocky bottom.

What little that I've wanted in life seems so far out of reach. Companionship. Security. Dignity.

As a 17-year-old I should be looking forward to a future glittering with happiness and possibilities. Instead, my world seems empty of what I need. A home. A way forward. And hope.

But somehow I know that if I don't give up on myself, if I avoid the deadly traps that have taken away girls in my situation, I can prove everyone wrong. That I am worthy. That I can succeed.

Tomorrow barely glows, but it does glow.

All I have to do is survive.

# CHAPTER TWO

You would think that Jamaica would've been a paradise for any young child. There was so much open land and so much coastline and for most of the year, a wonderfully pleasant climate that attracts so many tourists to our island home. But for me, those childhood days were often anything but paradise. And I have my maternal grandmother, Dorcas Kelly, and my father Ricardo to blame for those painful memories.

Since my mother Sadie worked as a domestic helper in Kingston, my sister Primrose, my brother Paul, and I stayed with Grandmother Dorcas. My father managed Bailey's Funeral Home in Santa Cruz, which was closer than Kingston, but he couldn't be trusted to take care of us on account of his fondness for the bottle.

\*\*\*

"Petergay!" Grandmother Dorcas yanked my hair. "Child, hold still."

Today was Sunday, supposedly the day of rest and a time to reflect on God's blessings. But for me there was no rest from Grandmother's torments, nor was it a blessing to be suffering at her hand. Even though I was four years old, I was well aware that

Grandmother was punishing me to get back at my father, whom she despised, but couldn't act against.

We were getting ready for church. I was already in my best Sunday clothes and kneeling in front of my grandmother where she sat in a chair, my back to her so she could arrange my hair. "Look at this nappy mess I have to fight with." The comb's teeth scraped across my scalp. She yanked again. Tears welled in my eyes and though I tried to keep quiet, I let out a squeak of pain.

"What are you complaining about?" She boxed my ear, which only made me cry. "I'm the one doing all the work. Everything about you is like your father. He's a drunken wreck and you'll be no better," she said with another tug on my hair, and proceeded to again remind me how much I looked like him, from my dense curly hair, to my dark skin, to my very African features. Paul and I were both my father's children, but as Paul was the firstborn on my mother's side, he was Grandmother's favorite. She stabbed the comb into my hair, the teeth digging to the scalp, and she twisted her wrist to snag another pull.

Sometimes though, she was gentle, but that didn't mean I was out of harm's way. On those occasions, the delicate caressing of my hair would relax me to the point that I'd start to snooze.

Then a hard slap against my head would jolt me awake.

"Miserable child," she scolded, "don't you dare fall asleep on me."

\*\*\*

We lived in a typical Jamaican home for people who didn't have much money. The house was a simple dwelling with one room, an outside makeshift kitchen, and the outhouse.

Meals were another opportunity for my grandmother to pile on the abuse. At mealtimes, we sat in a circle on the floor. The smell of burning wood from the stove hung in the air. She ladled healthy portions into the bowls of my brother and sister, giving them big, tasty servings of meat and vegetables. Grandmother carefully spooned out what she gave to me, which were scraps, mostly thin gravy and tough gristle, barely enough to keep my stomach from grumbling. The vegetables in my bowl were nothing but stems and pulp. I had learned long ago not to complain, because if I did, she'd whisk my bowl off the table and dump it outside. Then she'd slap my face and say, "Child, you are as ungrateful as you are ugly. If you get hungry, maybe the dogs will share."

It was seldom that I satisfied my appetite with dinner. I waited in hope for another helping, because even this gruel was better than trying to sleep with hunger pangs.

After the meal, she would order me, "Collect the dishes." While I gathered the dishes and put them in the washbasin, she fried dumplings on the stove. Paul, her favorite got two, Primrose got one, and Grandmother made it a point to show that I got nothing.

That's what I meant to her, nothing.

\*\*\*

The holidays provided no respite from my humiliations. One Christmas, Grandmother's husband brought us gifts. Paul received a toy police car and Primrose and I got small dolls.

We were sitting on the floor and playing with our toys when Paul demanded, "Let me have your doll. I want to give her a ride in my police car."

"No," I protested and clutched my doll. I was seldom given presents so this toy was a treasured possession.

He tried to grab it, and we ended up on the floor, wrestling for my doll, and yelling for the other one to let go.

Grandmother charged into the room from outside. She saw me fighting with her favorite grandchild, and so in her mind, whatever the problem was, it was my fault. Seizing my arm, she lifted me from Paul. She tore the doll from my hand and tossed it to my brother. Then she slapped me, squeezed my arm tighter, and slapped me again.

I wailed at the pain and the injustice.

"Shut your mouth," Grandmother cursed as she kept slapping me. I broke out of her grip to crawl away but she snatched my blouse and dragged me to her. My resistance only stoked her rage and she spanked me with greater fury. "Miserable child! Ungrateful brat!"

I scrambled against the floor as her blows landed across my backside. Tears gushed down my cheeks and mixed with the snot coming out of my nose. I knew I was a pathetic mess, but what could I do?

She let go and stood, breathing heavily from the effort of beating me. "Clean yourself up," she scolded and went outside.

Through blurry, tear-soaked eyes I looked at my brother and sister. They had watched, sympathetic but powerless. There was a set of rules for them, and another set for me. Their fate was to be pampered while it was mine to be punished simply for being who I was.

\*\*\*

Once, Grandmother pushed me down so hard that I hit the floor and bruised my hip. Picking myself up, the injury hurt so much that I had to hobble around.

That afternoon, my mother arrived on her day off. As she announced herself when close to the house, my siblings and I ran to her, shrieking with delight. She brought a tote bag filled with food and treats. We crowded around her for a group hug, then followed her into the house, happy as a brood of puppies. She noticed my limp. "Petergay, what's wrong with you?"

Living in Jamaica, one thing you learn from an early age is that there is nothing lower than a snitch. You never rat on someone, no matter what they've done. You cope by either living with the transgression or you get even. I was too small to get even with Grandmother Dorcas so I kept my anger and resentments to myself. Plus, I knew that if I told on Grandmother, what was to prevent her from taking revenge once Mother left?

"I was playing in the street and fell." I pointed out the door to give credence to my lie.

Mother warmed me with a sympathetic smile. "Child, you can be so clumsy." She regarded Grandmother. "Please watch over her."

"Sadie, I will do my best," Grandmother replied, her face innocently blank of menace. She was like a mean cat that had temporarily drawn its claws back. And once my mother left, those claws would be extended again and come swiping after me.

\*\*\*

The days my father dropped by my grandmother's house were never a cause for celebration. He'd only show up because he was either drunk or hungry.

Today he entered the house without knocking. He steadied himself against the doorframe and then eased into a chair. He was dressed in his work clothes, a white shirt over dark trousers, his tie loose. His attire told me he had come here directly, more or less, from his job at the funeral home.

"Where's Dorcas?" he demanded.

Paul and Primrose looked at him warily and retreated out the kitchen. I started to follow them when Father grabbed my arm. His fingers were like bands of iron. His breath smelled of hard liquor and his eyes were bloodshot. He glanced over his shoulders to make sure we were alone.

His grasp relaxed and his hand stroked my back. As I was getting older, he was touching me more and more but his attentions were hardly affectionate. I stiffened and my mouth went dry with dread as his hand ran along my hip. Breath whistled out his nostrils and his gaze narrowed as he regarded me with anticipation. I closed my eyes and prayed. *Please stop. Please stop.*

A noise from outside startled us and he pulled his hand away. Sighing in relief, I stepped from him.

His tone turned harsh. "Find me something to eat. It's almost lunchtime."

Grateful for the rescue from his clutches, I rummaged in the pantry and acted busy, knowing that I was forbidden from removing anything without Grandmother's permission.

"Petergay," she shouted, "what are you doing?"

I jumped from the pantry. "Father wants something to eat."

She was at the door and swiveled her spiteful gaze from me to him. As much as she despised him, she kept her distance. What protected her was that this was her house and he had no say. If he were to strike her, then the community would castigate and shun him. But even sober my father didn't have much common sense, and drunk, he was like a junkyard dog ready to bite you. You learned to keep clear of him.

Grandmother glared at him. "Why aren't you at work?"

Father crossed his arms and glared back. "I didn't come here to answer your questions." He reached for me and wrapped his arm around my waist. "I came to see how Petergay was doing."

His creepy touch made me want to run out of the kitchen.

Grandmother snorted in derision at his reply. "You see she's still here. Another mouth for me to feed. What else do you want?"

Father let me go. He leaned in his chair to peer into the open pantry. "Dorcas, how about lunch?"

"Food doesn't just appear in this house. You have money?"

Father dug into his pocket and offered her a wad of crinkled bills. Grandmother's mouth pruned with annoyance, but she took the money. As much as I detested them both, I enjoyed watching how they baited each other.

Father rubbed his chin as his eyes roamed about the room, indicating he was still looking for something to eat. I could tell he was considering his options. He had an agenda in coming here, and that was satisfying his hunger.

Then he said, "Dorcas," his voice turning sweet, "you're a good cook. You know that. Why should I go somewhere else when the best meals in Jamaica are right here?" He gave her a wide, sugary smile. When he had to be, my father could be as charming as he was otherwise bitter.

"Ricardo, I'm not buying what you're selling."

"I'm not selling anything."

"If I fix you a bowl, will you go?"

Seeing as he was getting his way, my father's smile beamed

brighter as he tracked her to the stove. "As long as it's a good meal."

"You'll have to eat whatever I give you." Grandmother stoked the wood inside the stove and then set a pot of food on top. As she stirred the pot, she ordered me to fetch a bowl. After the pot heated, she had me hold the bowl while she dumped rice and meat into it.

I handed the steaming bowl to Father, who set it on his lap. The food smelled wonderful, though I knew when it was my turn to eat, I wouldn't get as much. I gave him a spoon and he began shoveling the meal into his mouth. When he was done, he passed the bowl back to me and stood. The meal seemed to have sobered him a bit; still he left the house without thanking my grandmother.

The happiness that I felt at his departure didn't last long. Grandmother pinched my arm and twisted the skin. The pain forced me to my knees. "You're just like him, ugly child."

She let go and swatted my face. Hands raised to protect my head, I cowered like a punished dog, expecting more torment.

Grandmother didn't disappoint. She grabbed a spatula and proceeded to smack my arms and hands. Each blow made me whimper. I could do nothing but endure. If I tried to run away or take shelter under the table, she'd only beat me harder. As I cried, I wished that she would drop dead right on the spot. But I would have to wait years for that to happen.

# CHAPTER THREE

The happiest day of my life was when my grandmother Dorcas Kelly died.

There, I said it.

***

People say you are judged by the company you keep, but this isn't always true. Especially in the case of my grandmother and her good friend Miss Punsie, who was as generous as my grandmother was vindictive.

One Sunday afternoon, Miss Punsie was sitting on a chair in my grandmother's home. I enjoyed her visits as she always treated me with kindness.

She beckoned me to her. "Are you okay?" She wrapped an arm around my waist and pulled me against her leg. I wanted to jump into her lap and hug her.

I couldn't tell her the truth about what Grandmother and my father were doing to me. But Miss Punsie sensed that I was unhappy and always on edge. And she was astute enough not to ask Grandmother, who would surely deny anything was wrong, then beat me senseless once Miss Punsie had left.

Grandmother entered the room.

"Dorcas, I've a favor to ask," Miss Punsie said.

"There's no reason to ask," Grandmother replied, smiling. "Whatever you want, consider it done."

Miss Punsie stroked my shoulder. "I'd like Petergay to go with me to the market."

Grandmother's smile didn't fade a bit, but her eyes swiveled to me, wary and condemning. "Are you sure? Petergay can be a handful."

"It's a long walk and I'd like someone to talk to."

I couldn't believe Miss Punsie would need someone as young and small as me for company.

Grandmother regarded me with another sharp look, then met eyes with Miss Punsie and shrugged, as if her friend had no idea what she was getting into.

When Miss Punsie left, I walked close behind her. I could feel my grandmother's burning gaze, but I didn't bother to turn and see her expression. I didn't know if she was suspicious, or jealous, or relieved that I was out of her hair.

As we ambled down the road, past the other houses and the stands of trees, Miss Punsie told me stories from her childhood. I wasn't used to an adult talking to me this way, so openly, so graciously, and I felt so incredibly happy and free. All my problems seemed so far away.

From behind us we heard the buzz of a motorbike. We turned to see how close it was to us. The bike was still a ways from us, but I could see a large white box between its two front tires. The cheery ringing of a bell confirmed what I thought. This was the ice cream man making his Sunday rounds. Miss Punsie and I stepped to the side of the road to let him pass.

She reached into a skirt pocket and fished out some coins.

"Here," she passed the coins to me. "Get us something."

As the motorbike approached, it let loose an inviting ring from the bell. I waved my arm at the ice cream man and as he slowed, I showed him the money in the palm of my hand.

He pulled short of me and left the engine running, blue smoke putt-putting out the tail pipe. The sunlight shining off his sunglasses matched the reflection from his toothy smile. He leaned over the handlebars and opened the box's lid. Frosty air blasted out. I stepped close and rose on tiptoes to get a view inside the box. He sorted through the colorful boxes and selected a pair of frozen pops on wooden sticks. After picking the coins from my hand, he gave me the pops; one was red, the other orange. He snapped the box lid closed, gave me another broad smile, and puttered away.

Carefully, I carried the frozen pops to Miss Punsie. She led me to the shade under a large tree. I held up both pops for her to select one, but she told me to choose. This was so amazing. Rarely was I given a treat and even more rarely was I allowed to choose. Things were just given to me or I was told what to do.

I took the red one. Miss Punsie showed me how to peel loose the sticky paper wrapping. We sat beneath the tree and listened to a breeze rattle through its leaves. Everything seemed so tranquil and calm and I wondered why every day couldn't be like this.

I leaned against Miss Punsie, grateful that she was showing me that the world was capable of giving me kindness.

***

When I returned to Grandmother's, she didn't hesitate in letting me know that she was not only displeased, but also insulted that I had stayed with Miss Punsie.

Grandmother grabbed a handful of my hair and pulled me to my knees. "Ungrateful wretch." She slapped my face. "How dare you embarrass me in front of my friend."

Her blows rained upon me. I withered under the pain and humiliation. But each blow served to etch hatred deeper into my heart.

\*\*\*

Miss Punsie asked my parents if she could adopt me. Though I loved my mother, I knew that my circumstances would be better for me if I lived with Miss Punsie.

My mother was puzzled and a bit hurt by the request, as if Miss Punsie was implying that she was not doing a good job. Mother was being pulled in many directions by her responsibilities. She could only be at one place at a time and was guilt-ridden for not being always available for my siblings and me. But she could never let us go, and so she told Miss Punsie, no.

\*\*\*

Soon after that, several of my relatives and my mom began to visit my grandmother. We children were sent outside so that they could speak among themselves in hushed tones. Something terrible was happening.

Then my mother quit her job in Kingston and moved in with

my grandmother. Just like that, I was better treated. My meals improved and I didn't have to worry about my grandmother abusing me.

We kids soon learned what was the problem. My grandmother had been diagnosed with cervical cancer. I should've been overwhelmed with remorse, but I wasn't. Every Sunday we were told that God would punish evildoers, and to me there was no greater evildoer than Grandmother Dorcas. There was no doubt that I regarded her suffering as God's punishment for being such a cruel person.

On the day we laid her to rest, I acted sad like everyone else at the funeral, but inside I was smiling.

\*\*\*

As warm and accommodating as the weather can be, in the autumn Mother Nature would often turn on us. In early September 1988, we learned that Hurricane Gilbert was headed our way. Though we lived on higher ground with wooded hills between us and the sea, the adults cautioned that we could still suffer the storm's fury.

Nervously, we tracked the weather reports on the TV and the radio. Although everyone spoke in dire terms, to us kids it was exciting. When the weather reports confirmed that we were in the hurricane's path, people evacuated from the coast and packed the inland towns. All the birds disappeared, as did the stray dogs, replaced by police and government officials who were suddenly everywhere.

The grocery shelves were abruptly picked clean. A sense of

panic filled the air. We kids were told to fill as many containers with fresh water as we could and then store them in the house.

The skies boiled like gray pudding and the trees groaned as they were whipped by an ever-fiercer wind. According to the radio, the storm was almost right on top of us. Father and some of his friends nailed boards over our windows.

The sky grew dark and the rain fell like angry pellets. My mother called us inside the house to take shelter. We huddled inside, not convinced we were safe from the howling winds. The rain cascaded in sheets. Trash and tree branches were dragged along in the torrents of water flowing down the streets. The wind beat against the house, and at that moment I felt the pangs of terror. Sheets of plywood and corrugated tin skipped along the streets, ready to slice into anyone who dared to venture outside. It was like nature, through the hurricane, was gnawing away at everything we took for granted. She was in charge and letting us know it.

The house began to tremble, and we kids gathered around Mother like chicks seeking protection with their hen. The roof shook apart and rain sprayed down upon us. The water in the street reached the house and began chewing at the foundation.

The wind tore off more and more of the roof until rain poured into every corner of the house. I cried out in fear. Mother scurried about, valiant as she heaped our belongings under a tarp to keep them from getting ruined.

Then the wind died down, followed by the diminishing rain, which seemed to have wrung the storm clouds dry. An eerie quiet settled over the ruined landscape, the silenced punctuated by water dripping from roofs and trees. The streets were like rivers as the runoff rushed toward lower ground.

We stood outside, barefoot in the mud, our clothes soaked. A police truck plowed through the street, wheels-deep in the water. Electrical poles had been knocked down. Torn branches and odd pieces of houses littered the street.

Mother waded through the standing water as she surveyed the damage to our house and the neighborhood. I stayed close to her. Most of our roof was gone and the foundation was cracked. Our beds and other furniture were soaked.

The destruction seemed overwhelming, and I had no idea how we'd get things the way they were before. Father helped my mother collect our belongings.

"Petergay," my mother called. She handed me a basket. "We have work to do."

***

Our house was beyond repair so we moved in with Miss Rebecca Patterson, a friend of my parents. Her house survived the hurricane without much damage. To make room for us, she went to live with her son in Kingston, which meant our family had the large one-room house to ourselves. Plus, we had electricity and her kerosene stove.

Sometimes Miss Pat would invite me to spend the night with her. She would tuck me into bed and linger to tell me funny stories from her life. She then turned off the light, and I remained still, staring out the window toward the stars.

I could feel all the bad in my life running beneath me as if I hovered over it. At any moment, I could drop back into it and my life would return to its cruel self.

But the stars seemed to reach into me and fill me with a hope that my future would be filled with goodness. I wanted to cry, then scolded myself. *Why are you not being thankful for these moments of peace? Be grateful that Miss Pat is around to watch over you.*

The next morning, she served me a nice breakfast and spent several minutes taming my unruly hair, though doing it with a welcome tenderness.

For now it seemed that we had escaped catastrophe, but before I could breathe easier, my familiar troubles returned to torment me.

One afternoon I was alone in the house, on the bed I shared with my siblings. A shadow darkened the doorway and I could tell it was my father. I got tense. I wanted to believe that his showing up when I was alone was a coincidence. I heard him close the front door.

Sliding off the bed, I started to leave. But too late; he cut me off, giving me a smile twisted by drunkenness and vile thoughts. "Petergay," he said, his voice making me recoil.

Scooting onto the bed, I tried to put distance between us to show that he was unwelcome. But he sauntered in anyway. I sat against the wall and drew my legs to my chest. I avoided eye contact and stared at the bed covers just past my toes.

He settled onto the bed beside me, uninvited. The odor of his alcoholic breath made me gag. My skin crawled.

"You're growing up so fast." He put his hand on my knee and I was so overcome with nausea that I wanted to throw up.

He touched my hair. "Soon you'll be a young woman."

My head began to tremble. Whenever he did this, I felt dirty and used. I wanted to scratch him, bite him, hurt him. Anything to make him stop and go away.

He slid one hand down my thigh and I felt my insides curdle and go sour. I was trapped and sensed that the worst was about to happen.

Then the front door clicked open. My father bolted from the bed. As he walked out, he gave me a withering look that warned me to keep this between us.

\*\*\*

I wish that had been the last time that he tried to fondle me. Every time he was around me I grew sick with guilt, like I was inviting this anguish upon myself. If I told anyone what was happening they would either not believe me, or condemn me for not keeping quiet about family secrets.

As I grew out of adolescence, I could feel my body changing and I knew I was making myself more tempting to the depraved advances from my father. Whenever I thought we'd be alone, I would leave the house. But that wasn't always possible.

My mother was frequently gone during the day, working. I'd be at home, safely accompanied by my siblings. Then I'd look up and see that they were gone. At that point, I'd realize my father was home, just him and me, like he had planned it. As usual he'd be drunk and start to ogle me with crazy, lust-filled eyes. He'd talk to me real sweet-like as if I had no idea of what was on his mind. Then he'd seize my arm and push me into a corner, or he'd force me onto a bed. In any case, he'd tower over me, his stinking breath announcing what was in his heart. I clenched my arms across my chest, and cried out for him to leave me alone. He'd paw me, his big hands sliding over my backside and along the inside of my thighs.

My protests only seemed to stoke his desire. He'd wrench my wrists apart and struggle to get his hands inside my blouse.

Fortunately, someone or something would interrupt him. He'd retreat, grinning, certain that sooner or later, he'd get his way.

***

One morning I had enough, and ran away to stay with an older friend, Verona. I felt especially safe with her because she and her husband, Raulston, were active in their church. As dutiful Christians, every Sunday morning they left to attend the worship services. I stayed home as I didn't belong to their church and if I appeared there, people would start asking questions I didn't want answered.

One Sunday, Raulston complained of a headache and stayed in bed. A half hour after Verona left, he called me to his bedroom, and I went, thinking he needed me to fetch him aspirin or make tea. When I approached his bed, he snatched my arm and pulled me on top of him. Groping wildly, he tried to rip off my blouse and jeans. I yelled and fought back hard, finally pulling loose and running out of the bedroom.

I remained in the kitchen, shaking all over and cold with fright. I eyed a knife by the sink in case he came after me.

About the time that Verona was due home, Raulston went outside and waited for her. When she arrived, he greeted her. I realized what he was doing. He was getting onto her good side before she saw me. Sure enough, when they came into the house, she acted happy that her husband was up and doing better.

I didn't know how to ease into what had happened so I simply blurted, "Raulston tried to rape me."

Before I could explain, Raulston yelled, "Are you crazy? Rape you?" He put his arm around Verona.

Her surprised gaze cut from me to her husband and to me again.

"This girl is nothing but trouble." Raulston stabbed his finger at me. "Why is she here anyway? What good girl runs away from her home?"

"Why would you say this, Petergay?" Verona asked.

Raulston jumped between us. "I'll tell you why. She's jealous. She sees what a good thing we have here and she wants to ruin it."

I was speechless. Raulston glared at me, fuming. Verona regarded me with her large, searching eyes. He stepped back and hugged her. My silence was condemning me, but nothing I could say would help.

Verona sighed. "Petergay, I think that it's best that you go."

Falsely accused, I was crushed. It seemed that everywhere that I went, I was marked as prey for the men, while the women stood by and did nothing. I forced back tears and gathered my things into a bag. Where would I go?

Just as I was about to leave, Verona asked, "When you get home, I need you to give this to Sandra." Sandra was a mutual friend.

I had no intention of returning home. Reluctantly, I took the envelope, thinking that Verona was being quite cheeky in asking for a favor as she's kicking me out of her home.

When I passed through the farmer's market I ran into Karen, who was an acquaintance of Sandra and me. Since Karen knew her, she could deliver the envelope and save me the risk of running into my father. I made my request to Karen.

"Why don't you do it?" she asked.

"You'll probably see her first."

27

Karen pocketed the envelope, and we parted ways.

From there I found my Uncle Frank and stayed with him a few days before spending time at a cousin's, then with a friend. I was surrounded by a vast community but had no place to call sanctuary. I couldn't return home because sooner or later, my father would overpower me. Even if I fought like a wild animal and did everything possible to protect myself, I knew I'd be branded with shame if he got his way.

One afternoon I was on my way to the store when Verona saw me.

"Thief!" she yelled.

I shrank from her, confused by her accusation.

She ran up to me, her eyes burning with rage and betrayal. "You stole my money."

"What are you talking about?"

"There was a hundred and fifty dollars in that envelope you promised to give to Sandra."

Instantly I knew what had happened. Karen had taken the money. Had I looked into the envelope I would've seen the money and then delivered it straightaway to Sandra. But without proof, I had no way to deflect Verona's allegations.

"Thief!" Verona screamed, loud enough to draw a crowd.

I withdrew from their collective stare of condemnation and hurried away from Verona. She screamed louder and I ran faster.

It seemed that there was no place on the island where I was safe from injustice and violation.

# CHAPTER FOUR

Let me explain how I lived during my adolescence to my early teenage years. I'd run away for a few days, return home, have my father attempt to molest me, and I'd then take off again. Because I kept the problems between my father and me to myself, people assumed I was the troublemaker and that's the reason I stayed away from home.

One activity that kept me grounded was school. I enjoyed the routine, having fun with my schoolmates, and learning new things that opened my eyes to the world beyond our little island. My teacher, Miss Smith, appreciated my curious nature and that I was a quick study.

A classmate, Carlene, and I became good friends. She invited me to her home and that's where I met her older brother, Mark. I was 15 and at that stage in a girl's life when she gets a little boy-crazy. Mark was cute and charming. His attentions made me feel special and desirable. His touch excited me and I was pleased how much it thrilled him when I touched him as well. We all lived in similar circumstances, small houses without much privacy. Yet we managed to sneak around and have fun together.

As I grew to like him more and more, we became that much more intimate. We were so misinformed about sex that I had no idea what we were doing could get me pregnant.

After a few weeks of this intimate behavior I started to not feel well. When I got up in the morning I'd be queasy. Sometimes I'd get so nauseous that I threw up. I'd have bouts of moodiness, mostly sadness, and at school I had problems paying attention to my lessons.

Miss Smith noticed my unusual behavior and took me aside. After asking a few general questions about my health, she then suggested that I get a medical examination. I didn't ask her what she thought the problem was, but I knew something was seriously wrong with me.

Out of her own pocket, she paid for my doctor's visit. During the examination, I was both nervous about my health condition and at the same time, hopeful that the doctor could offer a cure. Miss Smith joined me when the doctor shared his diagnosis.

I was pregnant.

With that announcement, it's like the world had given way beneath me. In one instant, my world had collapsed and everything about my future had changed.

Aside from that, I didn't know how I was supposed to feel or react. I was not ready to be a mother and be responsible for a child; after all, I was a child myself, still a young teenager. What did I know about being a mother? I had taken care of plenty of babies, but I could walk away from those chores. This baby was mine to watch over forever.

This new future draped me with dark uncertainties. My mind was a jumbled mess, and I had trouble assembling my thoughts, much less putting words together.

I sensed that I was on the edge of great peril, like walking on a high wire where everybody could see me, and they expected me to fall. Everything about the moment felt so wrong, like I had done a terrible thing. Somehow, I wanted to undo what had happened. As bad as my life could be before I was pregnant, I'd rather be there than in the situation where I was now.

Miss Smith visited the market to speak with my mother. I imagined her telling Mother that I was pregnant and the shock registering on Mother's face. I knew my mother would ask, how was Miss Smith so certain. Miss Smith would answer that she and I had just come back from the clinic.

Later, when Mother returned home I read her disappointment in me, and that made me want to cry. Her gaze seemed to see right through me like an x-ray as if she was looking for the baby. She wiped her nose, and her eyes became shiny. She was close to crying and that made the tears well up even more in my eyes. Mother had done so much for me, and I had let her down. I felt like such a bad person.

She remained deep in thought about this new predicament I had brought into the house, as if she didn't have enough worries.

I went outside, stayed close to the house for a few minutes, then walked around the neighborhood, my stomach rumbling with hunger. As much as I would lose my appetite in the morning, in the afternoon I'd be ravenous. Then it seemed there was no limit to what I could eat. I realized why; I was now eating for two.

*I am pregnant*, I kept repeating. *Like it or not, I am going to be a mother.*

Placing my hands over my belly, I thought that I might be able to feel the baby growing inside me. It was if my body was no longer mine. As the day grew late I was getting hungrier and returned home, wondering what Mother had prepared for dinner.

As I rounded the corner and my house came into view, I saw

my father braced against the doorway. He was standing erect and appeared fully sober.

We made eye contact. His expression burned with rage and he stormed toward me.

Hands balled into fists, he marched close, his face a withering scowl. I halted, uncertain, afraid even, of what violence he was capable of.

Standing over me, he let loose a string of curses. I shrank from him, afraid that he was going to hit me.

"You're worthless," he screamed and blocked my way to the house. "What kind of a girl gets herself pregnant? What kind of a grandchild are you giving me?"

I couldn't believe his questions. I was the one in trouble and yet, he only saw my situation as it affected him.

As it was, at any given moment I was always swinging from mood to mood. With him screaming at me like this, I was pushed into a state of complete vulnerability. I started to cry, which only stoked his temper. I wished that he was liquored up. Though a mean drunk, when he'd had too much the alcohol diluted his strength and wit. But sober, his mind was razor sharp and he wielded his words like knives.

"How can you do this to me? Getting yourself pregnant," he hollered loud enough for the neighborhood to overhear. People circled close, drawn by the drama at my expense.

I started to step around my father, when he blocked my path. "Where do you think you're going?"

I was trembling with fear. It took much strength for me to reply. "Home," I answered meekly.

"You have no home," he bellowed. "You're dead, you just don't know it."

# CHAPTER FIVE

Fifteen and pregnant, that was me.

Except for Miss Smith, I didn't tell anyone at school that I was going to have a baby. Still, my dad's public outburst when he found out about my condition made sure that the neighborhood knew. From there, it didn't take long for everyone in the school to know that I was pregnant and for them to wag their tongues in disapproval. Good girls in Jamaica didn't get pregnant, only the bad ones who couldn't control themselves.

The situation was an ugly double standard because Mark, the child's father, suffered no recriminations. In fact, he was seeing other girls, and they didn't hesitate to skewer me with looks of disdain as if I was unworthy of him or of being in their presence.

With each new week I began to show, which only provoked more stares and gossip. My breasts were getting fuller and my belly more swollen. Day by day, my sense of disgrace increased, and there was nothing I could do to hide what I was going through.

Despite my frail condition, my father didn't let up with his insults and torments. I'd wake up nauseous with morning sickness and rather than offer empathy or understanding—not that I expected any from him—he'd pile on the rebukes.

I became the school pariah. One by one my schoolmates

shunned me. The glares and the whispers of condemnation grew more pointed and sharp.

My school uniform grew tighter until at five months, it barely fit. And this made matters for me even worse. If I went to school wearing regular clothes, that would have me stand out even more and make it more obvious that I was different and why. The day that I could no longer fit into my uniform, that's when I decided not to attend school anymore.

My situation fueled a worsening depression. I enjoyed learning and knew that an education was key to my getting ahead in the world. But my pregnancy had become a door that was slammed in my face, blocking me of opportunities. And all that was wrong in my life seemed like it was my fault, that I was being punished for being naive about sex.

I spent my days at home, helping my mother keep the house. Miss Smith would send, via my siblings, extra food, assorted baby clothes, and books and pamphlets to explain what I was going through. Being pregnant seemed so complicated, and it was, but Mother Nature was taking care of the details as she had since the beginning of history.

Every time I left the house I'd feel people watching, judging, condemning. It seemed that my shame gave everyone plenty to talk about, as if my disgrace was public entertainment. Some people went out of their way to mumble insults or more brazenly, shout them to my back. People would smirk and sneer, as if they were too good for me.

I felt so alone. I knew other girls had gone through this; after all I wasn't the first young woman to have a baby out of wedlock. *Wedlock*, there was even a special word to describe my situation.

Did it have to be this way? What if Mark and I had gotten married? Would people regard me any differently? I had no answer. But such thoughts were idle musings that did nothing to help me. Mark would never marry me—he was eight years older than I was—and still a boy despite his boastful posturing. In any case, he was too young to be a provider, plus the way he distanced himself from me only revealed the true nature of his shallow character.

With each passing day, it was as if the world was squeezing me. Sometimes I couldn't breathe, I felt so trapped. Getting out of bed each morning was like turning a blind corner and finding myself further and further from where I wanted to be: an independent woman, strong and proud, prosperous and accomplished.

I was so wrapped in my gloomy thoughts that the first time I felt the baby kick, I was astounded by the reality of what was happening to me. Sure, I knew that I had another human being growing in my belly, but so far, that condition was about how it affected my outward appearance and station in life. The morning sickness had stopped, so now I woke up famished. Quite suddenly, I'd get cravings, and I never had a problem finishing my meals.

I was lying in bed when that first kick happened. It startled me so much that I cried out in surprise. I pulled up my t-shirt to expose my naked belly, now the size of a watermelon. Laying a hand on my belly, I wanted to see if I could feel the baby move.

And I did! Small bones pushed against the inside of my belly.

I was amazed that another human being was growing inside me. I cupped my swollen belly with both hands and stared at it.

For the first time since becoming pregnant, I was warm with love and pride. No one else in the world could do what I was doing, nurturing this particular baby. My responsibilities were real.

I needed to take care of myself. So far, I was doing pretty good at that. I didn't smoke or drink or take drugs. I ate as best I could.

I wondered if the baby was a boy or a girl and what he or she would look like. What part of the baby would look like me and what part would look like Mark? I noted that for some reason boys tended to resemble their mother and girls their father.

Stroking my belly, I talked to my baby, certain that he or she heard me. I promised this small gift that I would be the best mother ever.

But I couldn't ignore my situation. I had no way to provide for the baby, and my father made it clear that I was not welcome to be under the same roof as him. When my place at home became too oppressive, I'd visit Miss Smith and sit on her porch where we'd talk.

One matter that occupied my mind was what to name the baby. I became fascinated with names and tried various ones on my baby as if they were clothes. I ran through name after name and discarded them in turn. Some names sounded goofy. Others, I appreciated how they sounded, but if they were already given to someone I didn't like, then I'd forget them. My baby's name had to be special. A name should inspire your child to be a good person and to do great things.

So my mind was always aware of names, even if I was doing something else. One afternoon I was watching television and when the end credits of the movie started to roll, I scanned through the list of names. Then I saw one: Alrick.

Instantly, I knew that name was perfect and that's what I chose for my baby if it was a boy.

During my eighth month, I was so big that I'd waddle from my home to the clinic for a checkup. I was already self-conscious of my large size, and my opinion of myself wasn't helped by the rebukes and looks of disgust that followed me whenever I went outside. By this time I imagined that I took up the entire street, so decided to no longer walk out in public and instead, I stayed home.

My mother kept an emotional distance from me until I was six months pregnant. After all, she had enough problems of her own. But as she remembered her first pregnancy, and knowing that I was unsure of what to expect, she began to take care of me. She marked the calendar and noted the days to my expected day of delivery. When I didn't feel well, she brought tea and held my hand. Whatever the unfortunate circumstances that had put me in this state, she was reaching out, mother to mother-to-be.

We made predictions about the baby's gender. One wives' tale said that carrying a baby high meant a boy. Another said a girl. Salt cravings meant a boy. Sweet cravings, a girl. But some days I craved potato chips and other days I craved ripe fruits and candy, so did this mean I would have both a boy and a girl? If I slept on my right side, it meant a boy. On my left, a girl. But that was hardly convincing, since I'd preferred to sleep on my right side since long before I was pregnant.

As ostracized as I was by most everyone, my sister Primrose did show some empathy and curiosity. Like our mother, she shared wives' tales about whether I was to have a boy or a girl. By dangling a charm over my belly, she claimed that if it swung back-and-forth I'd have a boy. If the charm made a circle, then I was to expect a girl. On some days it swung back-and-forth, and on others, it made a circle, so go figure.

When I first learned that I was pregnant, the actual birth

seemed distant, but now, with my belly so large it was lined with stretch marks and my navel pushed out, the inevitable reality was getting close. Mother filled me in about the labor contractions and the breaking of my water.

I asked if those would hurt.

"The water breaking is a popping sensation. But the contractions hurt a lot. Be ready."

At least she was being honest, though her explanations did little to ease my fears. I had nightmares of the baby splitting me open, or of a breech birth, or of the baby coming out in pieces, or deformed. There was no limit to what my imagination conjured to frighten me.

One spring evening my contractions began. Panicked, I called to my mother. She rushed to my side, alarmed by the news however expected. She flicked on the lights and I blinked into the glare.

"How are the contractions?" she asked.

"C-C-Coming," was all I could say.

I lay on my back, my legs apart. I pulled my t-shirt over my abdomen for my mother to see my belly trembling and changing shape.

The contractions came in painful waves, and the anxiety and effort of the labor drenched me in sweat. She moistened a towel and draped it on my forehead.

"Take off your panties," she said.

I tried, but I was so stiff from the contractions that I couldn't reach them and so she pulled them off me.

She had made arrangements with a neighbor to have his car ready to rush me to the hospital. Not that he or his wife cared about me, but my mother was well regarded in our community and they helped as a favor to her.

Mother hustled out of the house and I remained in bed, the contractions grinding through my lower back to my abdomen. To relieve the pain, I slid out of bed and walked around the room. When another contraction gripped me, I leaned against the wall to hold myself upright.

Then my water broke. It was as my mother had said. I felt the amniotic sac rupture and its fluid gushed from between my legs and onto the floor. I was so embarrassed, but more than anything, I was terrified. My body no longer seemed like it was mine. My lower back muscles spasmed and my insides throbbed. The baby kicked and shifted. The contractions grew stronger and more frequent.

I was overcome with misgivings. What if my mother didn't get back in time? What if the baby started to come out now? What would I do? If something bad were to happen to the baby I could never forgive myself.

The beams from car headlamps raked through the window. My back stiff with pain, I shambled to the door but was too overcome with more contractions to open it.

Mother burst inside, a whirlwind of activity. She took my arm and led me to the neighbor's car where it rumbled, waiting.

From this point, the night was a blur of pain and uncertainty, but a few random moments were captured clear as snapshots. I remembered the jostling ride in the car and that I was foolishly worried about my water breaking again and soiling the upholstery. Then I recalled arriving at the hospital and a nurse ushering me inside.

I remembered my mother and the nurse removing my t-shirt and helping me climb naked onto a birthing bed. My ankles settled into icy-cold steel stirrups.

Mother grasped my hand and we locked fingers. Every time a contraction wracked my body, I clamped down on her fingers. Consumed by agony, I stared at the ceiling and sucked at air. Glancing to one side, I saw in a mirror that the doctor had dragged a stool between my legs.

"Push," Mother commanded.

Eyes closed, I clenched my teeth and pushed hard, summoning strength I didn't know I had. I kept hearing more commands to push, but everything got lost in the chaos of pain and sensations coursing through my lower torso.

"There it comes," the doctor announced.

"Keep pushing, Petergay," my mother prompted as if I were in a race.

I concentrated on the tearing sensation between my legs. I felt the baby move through a tunnel of pain until…

"A boy," the doctor exclaimed.

With that, a loud beautiful shriek echoed through the room.

All eyes turned to the baby. The doctor tied off and snipped the placental cord, then handed my boy to the nurse, who wiped him clean and weighed him. The doctor tended to me and afterwards, the stirrups were lowered. My mother lifted my head and arranged pillows under my shoulders. She and the doctor covered me with a blanket.

The nurse brought my baby close. He was an angry curl of arms and legs, and his wrinkled face shrieked in protest at having been wrenched from my comfortable womb. She rested him on my chest and immediately he began squirming for my breasts. I lowered the blanket and pressed him to a nipple, which he began sucking.

The pain, the drama, all that ebbed and it felt like a terrible fever had broken. The sensation of my healthy son suckling from my breast filled me with an amazing joy. I etched the date into my memory: Wednesday, April 15, 1992.

"Have you chosen a name?" the nurse asked. "For the birth record."

"Alrick," I whispered, and spelled it out.

"Beautiful name," she replied. "He'll do you proud one day."

I was certain of this. Yesterday, it was only me. Now it was we. Alrick and me.

***

Returning home, Mother led me back to bed, where I collapsed, exhausted. My family and even neighbors, who had been relentless in castigating me, came by to visit, curious about the new addition to our household. Surprisingly, people wished me well. Perhaps the world was not such a bad place after all.

On occasion, I would take the baby to Miss Smith. "Such a splendid present from God," she'd tell me.

Little Alrick became a community project. Everyone acted as if he was special and an omen of good tidings. Even Mark stopped by to play with his son.

People treated me with deference. I ate well enough and had plenty of helpers to watch over the baby as I recovered.

Considering all the grief my father had given me during my pregnancy, he acted pleased with his first grandson. I wasn't sure my father would've been so welcoming if I had birthed a girl.

It wasn't long before my father returned to stoke his grudge against me. As usual with him, alcohol would fuel his resentments with the world and he'd focus his bitterness on me. He would get short and call me all kinds of names. I knew that soon something very bad would explode between us.

One afternoon he was particularly drunk and grumpy, and I recognized that I had to give him plenty of space, as much as I could, considering that my baby and I lived there as well.

But that did little to protect me. Father cursed and pushed me against the floor. I landed hard and struggled to get up.

"Get out," he shouted.

Sadness, betrayal, and anger boiled inside me. My heart pounded like it wanted to tear out of my chest. There was no limit to my father's hatred of me.

Knowing that I could barely survive on my own, I had no choice but to leave my baby behind.

As I shrank down the street, he hurled insults at me. "You're a no-good daughter and a no-good mother."

I retreated from him, not broken, but determined to prove him wrong. I hadn't ruined my life. I'd be back, with plenty of money, and after proving myself worthy to the world, I would reclaim my son.

# CHAPTER 6

I'd run away from home and was alone. At first, I was consumed with hatred for my father and sickened by the injustice that I was forced to suffer. But there was no one to turn to for help, least of all the authorities.

When I left home the sun was bright, and the hot, humid weather only added to my misery. I had no plans other than getting through my despair. It seemed like I had no long-term future. I visited the homes of friends and relatives who were kind enough to spare a meal and a bed to spend the night. People do this in Jamaica, since you never know when it will be your turn to ask for help.

But nothing comforted me. When I closed my eyes, all I could see was my son. What kept me from completely giving up on myself was the certainty that someday, in some way, he'd be back in my arms.

The circle that I wandered seemed to get wider and wider until I ended up in Kingston. What drew me was an older cousin, Deeta. I had heard she was doing all right for herself so I hoped she could provide some encouraging advice and a nudge in the right direction.

It turned out Deeta owned a bar where she introduced me to

several of her friends, all girls not much older than me. They were well-dressed, sporting lots of jewelry and fancy watches. They worked as dancers at Flippers, a local go-go club, which was what we called a strip club in Jamaica. I was amazed that they did whatever they pleased and smoked and drank without regard to what anyone thought of them.

I was young and naive about much in life. But desperate as I was to earn my keep, I was horrified about the idea about taking off my clothes in front of strangers, no matter how much money I was offered. Despite my reservations about their livelihood, these girls warmed up to me right away and took me into their fold as family. Two of them, Pamela and Nicole, were especially friendly and treated me like a younger sister.

They shared a nearby apartment and I was invited to stay with them while I figured out what to do next. Once in their apartment, Pamela played a record and they began to dance.

"Join us," Nicole said.

I didn't hesitate and got right among them, shaking and stepping to the beat. This was the first fun I'd had in a long time, and I was beside myself with joy.

The girls lit cigarettes and waved them as they danced, twirling smoke. Nicole puffed on a joint and passed it about the room, filling the room with more smoke and a weedy fragrance. When the marijuana was offered to me, I politely declined, as I had with the cigarettes. I felt uncomfortable refusing, since these girls were going out of their way to make me feel welcome and here I was putting limits on the hospitality I was willing to accept.

"Petergay, you have some nice moves," Nicole said. "You could make some good money."

"It's easy," Pamela added. "Just do what you're doing now. Only do it on stage. Like this." She jumped beside me and began to shimmy and shake while we all shrieked in approval.

But they didn't pressure me to dance at the club. Apparently, they understood that I was new to all this, and they had each been in my situation.

When it was time to leave for work, they changed into evening clothes.

Pamela opened her armoire. "Petergay, you and I are about the same size. Pick out something nice for yourself."

I had never worn such a pretty dress. We left in a group, Nicole and I arm-in-arm. As we strutted down the street, cars slowed for the passengers to gawk at us. Men shouted catcalls.

Pamela sneered in disapproval at one solicitation. "A date with you? You have no money, and besides, you're too old! Try asking my grandmother."

We laughed, defiant and haughty as spoiled princesses.

Arriving at Flippers, we approached the club through the alley entrance, which was unlocked and guarded by an enormous bouncer.

"Who do we have here?" He set his big, dark eyes on me. He was thick, like the trunk of a tree, with arms the size of telephone poles.

"Petergay is one of the new girls," Nicole explained.

"Tell me when she's dancing, and I'll make sure to watch."

I didn't correct him that I wasn't going to, since being one of the girls was the reason he was letting me in.

When we crossed the threshold into the club, we were treated to a refreshing blast of air conditioning. We were entering through the storage room, which was packed with crates of beer or bottles of liquor, and continued to a short, darkened hall and then the dressing room. Its door was hooked open and it looked as if it hadn't been closed in a long time. I guessed you couldn't expect any privacy while working here.

As the girls crowded into the room and began to change into their costumes, a lanky, older man by the door checked off their names. Pamela made the introductions. He was Andre, the club owner, and bore a leathery, wrinkled complexion. Considering he was looking at an assortment of young women in various states of undress, he didn't appear particularly impressed.

Pamela remarked, "Petergay wants to see what it's like to work here."

He gave me the once-over like I was for sale. "All right. Make sure that Pamela squares you with the rules before you do anything."

She asked if I wanted to see the club and took me back into the hall where we approached a black velvet curtain. She parted it for me to scope out the main room. It was dark save for the glow from neon signs scattered about the walls and the light from the bar at the far end. There wasn't really a stage but three platforms about shoulder height, each with steps to climb on top. Small cocktail tables had been arranged around the platforms.

American rock-n-roll music spilled from loudspeakers hanging from the ceiling. Everything about this place seemed so exotic and unworldly. The ambience was like I'd entered a forbidden lair.

But slowly, the artificially chilled air began to smell like an ashtray, and of stale liquor and mildew. The faint odor added an unsavory dimension to this fantasy world, where all you had to do was dance naked and you'd be showered with money.

We returned to the dressing room. The tight space was packed as more girls filed in and jostled for position in front of the mirrors to apply makeup and fix their hair. Many were topless as they unabashedly changed out of street clothes and into skimpy outfits. They were chatty and the mood was one of festive anticipation. Not many of them seemed to notice me, so that gave the impression that new girls were constantly cycling through the club.

The music abruptly changed and got louder. Nicole and two other girls in go-go costumes pushed past us and readied themselves at the curtain. When an overly cheery voice announced Nicole, she pranced into the main room.

I slipped through the curtain to stand along a side wall to watch. About twenty men were scattered about the room. Nicole climbed onto the middle platform, which was centered under the intense glare of spotlights. Her sequined outfit sparkled as if she were a living ornament.

Men appeared from a door that led from the entrance. They fumbled in the darkness, got their bearings, and made their way to the bar or a table. They arrived alone or in groups. Some immediately claimed chairs close to the platforms to give them a more intimate view. The flare of matches and cigarette lighters illuminated faces that glowed surreal and disembodied in the gloom. I watched and listened as they ordered drinks and settled in.

Fascinated, I studied the spectacle. The men didn't hesitate to pay triple the street price for drinks, this on top of the cover charge paid at the door, simply for the chance to watch women take off their clothes.

A few of the men, regulars I assumed by the way they spoke to Nicole, eagerly offered money, which she allowed them to slide under her garter belt. Or she parted her skirt so the men could tuck the money in her G-string underneath.

As the song continued, Nicole removed her skirt in a slow tease, then her blouse, until she was dancing in a tiny bikini top and the G-string. She made eye contact with several of the patrons to encourage offers of more money.

When the second song started, another girl appeared to take the platform to the far right. To keep attention on herself, Nicole undid her top in a slow reveal and let it fall to her feet. She danced topless, shimmying her breasts or bending over the men to let them dangle just out of reach. The men waved dollar bills that brought her to crouch close so they could slide money into what was left of her clothing. By the end of the song, she wore a garland of bills around her waist and each thigh.

When the third song started, she gathered all the money from her G-string and tucked the fistfuls of cash into her garters. She shimmied out of her G-string and I watched engrossed at how casual she seemed with her nakedness.

When the music tapered off, another girl was waiting to climb on the platform. Nicole collected her clothes and clambered down, sweat glistening on her face. She hustled out of the main room to disappear through the curtain. I rushed to join her.

By the time I had caught up to her, she was handing over her money to Andre, who guarded the threshold into the dressing room. He acted oblivious that she was naked as his attention was focused on the money she was counting into his hand.

After Nicole had given him the last of her money, she retreated to a corner of the dressing room and lit a cigarette.

Nicole turned her face toward a fan that swiveled from a bracket high on the wall. "I should take home three thousand dollars easy." We were talking about Jamaican dollars, which was about thirty dollars American.

My head swam with this information. My mother worked herself raw for two weeks to earn that amount of cash.

Pamela took her turn dancing. More girls kept filing into the dressing room. At four in the morning Nicole and Pamela quit dancing, tired but satisfied with their night's haul. We returned to the apartment.

A couple of days later, Pamela took me aside. "Petergay, you need to help around here."

"I'll be glad to help keep the place clean. Wash clothes."

Pamela shook her head. She raised her right hand and rubbed her fingertips together, as in, *you need to contribute money.*

In other words, I had better start dancing.

Resigned to do whatever was necessary to earn money until I got my son back, I convinced myself that I could dance at the club. After all, I wasn't a better person than Pamela or Nicole or any of the other dancers. I could dance as well as they could, they just did it topless and then, naked.

That evening I accompanied the girls to Flippers, and I laughed along with them, pretending that my debut as a go-go dancer was no big deal. But my heart was tight with apprehension.

I selected an outfit, a red sequined number that shined like fantastic fish scales against my dark skin. Once I put the costume on and looked at myself in the mirror, I was overcome with shame. I thought about all the men in the audience. What was I signaling by appearing like this? By now I learned that many of the girls made extra money by having sex with the patrons.

Embarrassed, I wrapped a towel around myself and pulled it tight.

Andre herded me out of the dressing room and toward the curtain. He tugged at my towel. "What is this?"

I clamped my hands on the towel to keep it from slipping off. "I... I... I don't want my outfit to get dirty."

Andre shrugged and nudged me through the curtain.

When I stepped through, it wasn't just as if every eye in the room was on me, it was more like everyone that I had ever known was watching. And not just the men, but also my mother, Miss Pat, and Miss Smith. I became so embarrassed that I couldn't breathe.

I teetered in my high heels to the first platform, my hands still clutching the towel. The men around the platform greeted my approach with hungry, expectant stares, like the towel was part of my act. They said something but their words were lost in the blare of the music and the blood thumping in my ears. Hesitantly, I climbed onto the stage, my feet unsteady in the high heels that now seemed impossibly tall and awkward.

I stood, my head swimming in a blur of faces, tobacco smoke, and music. The spotlight on me was impossibly bright. I tried swaying to the music but my movements were stiff and awkward, as if it hurt to move.

"Take off the towel!" someone shouted.

"Come on, girl, we came here for a show."

My mouth went dry. The other girls were busy doing their numbers, and they shot dirty looks at me for spoiling the mood.

The humiliation was too much. Tears burned my eyes. I couldn't drop the towel. I hurried off the platform and hobbled through the curtain back to the dressing room. I retreated to a corner, ashamed, frightened, riddled with guilt. I had let my new friends down. I changed out of the outfit into my clothes and hurried from the club.

Again, my life had come crashing down all around me.

I had another cousin, Nova, also in Kingston, and I headed to her home, where she gladly received me.

Older than me by five years, Nova had a mess of wild hair, and even though I didn't know her well, she did have the reputation of hanging around shady characters. We settled onto her bed and watched television as we picked at dinner. Sometime around nine, a male friend of hers, Damien, dropped by. He had brought a bottle of rum and gladly poured it into our drinks while he helped himself to most of its contents. Damien pawed drunkenly at his pockets. "Nova," he drawled, "I'm out of smokes. Could you get me a package?"

He fumbled his wallet out and plucked out a couple of bills. I noticed that many more remained in his wallet. Nova took the money and left for the store.

Damien kept watch on the door as if he wanted to make sure Nova wouldn't suddenly return. Then he smiled at me, a familiar, predatory grin that made the room seem very small.

He scooted close to me on the bed. He reeked of booze, and his eyes were bleary and unfocused. His skinny arms moved in clumsy gestures. I could leave, but where would I go? I wasn't going to let this drunken lout chase me away from my night's shelter.

When he tried to drape an arm over my shoulder, I pushed him hard. He slipped off the bed and crumpled to the floor. He lay still and I wondered if he had knocked himself out. Carefully, I eased close in case this was a trick. I shook him and saw that he was breathing but very much unconscious. I shook him again, harder. But he remained passed out.

He filled me with disgust. Then an idea hit me. I dug out his wallet and counted his money: $4,700. And it was now mine. I folded the bills and stashed them in my jeans pocket, then tucked the wallet back into his pants.

When Nova returned, she regarded Damien with the same disgust I had. "C'mon," she said. "Help me get him out of here before he throws up."

We hoisted him to his feet and half-carried/half-walked him out the door and down the block, where we dumped him at the corner.

Nova let me stay the night. Early the next morning I left, since I didn't want to be there in case Damien returned.

I dropped in on another older relative, Deborah, and used some of my newly acquired money to buy groceries as an incentive for her to let me stay. That afternoon, her friend Joshua dropped by. Unlike Damien, Joshua was sober and he kept his wits about himself. He entered the room like he owned the place and claimed a chair to join us as we watched television.

He flashed a roll of money and peeled off five hundred dollars. He offered me the bills. "In case you get hungry later."

I took the cash, but his offer only heated the disgust and hatred I was feeling toward all men. He tried making small talk but I remained cool to him. I could tell that he was like every other man I'd known—he only wanted to use me.

At various times of the night, men came to the door. Joshua would get up and follow them outside for a brief moment, then return inside while making a show of pocketing money. I knew what he was doing; he was selling drugs.

A little after midnight, a car stopped outside and Joshua bid us goodbye. He beamed with forced charm and disappeared outside.

The next afternoon I left for a walk to give myself time to think alone. When I returned to Deborah's, she and Joshua were waiting for me.

They radiated an expectant mood. "Joshua likes you," Deborah said. "He'd like you to move in with him."

I knew what that meant. He wanted me as his live-in booty call.

"No," I replied defiantly.

Deborah puffed up like an angry cat. "Why not? He's got money. You'll live okay."

My self-respect wouldn't allow it. "No. I don't like him. He's trouble I want no part of."

Joshua whispered in Deborah's ear.

She nodded and grimaced. "Petergay, you're too stupid to recognize when people are trying to help you. You only think of yourself and you'll never better your situation in life. If you're not willing to help yourself, then don't expect us to."

Deborah pushed the front door open. "Get out."

# CHAPTER 7

As much as I wanted to stay away from my father, I couldn't forget my son. Through the family grapevine I'd hear about Alrick, how he was doing, how big he was getting, and what a fine boy he would grow into. Through that same grapevine I'd send word back to my brother Paul that I'd be visiting home.

During my walk back there, I'd daydream about Alrick and imagine what a beautiful life I'd make for him...once I got money. But the reality of getting that money was so far removed from my daily struggle to survive that I might as well think about visiting the moon.

On the day that I arranged to see my son, Paul would sneak him from the house. Paul would claim that he was taking the baby to a relative's home, which was true. What he didn't mention was that I'd be there as well.

This time, Paul and I met at my Aunt Josephine's house. When I arrived, she offered a meal and a measure of sympathy for my plight. She shared some of her stories as we waited for Paul. He hadn't committed to a specific time, but no matter, this was Jamaica and if something was supposed to happen, it eventually happened.

I kept watch out the door of my aunt's house. About an hour

after lunch, Paul appeared down the street. He was strolling casually and cradled Alrick in his arms.

My heart leapt to them, but I stayed put as I didn't want word to
spread that Paul was secretly bringing Alrick to me.

When Paul handed my son over, I couldn't hold back my tears
of joy. This little creature was mine and he deserved to be with me.
I rocked him in my arms, then set him on my lap and cooed play-
fully to him. I studied him and remarked how much he'd grown
since the last time I'd seen him. All my anxiety and bitterness evap-
orated from the warmth of the love I felt for Alrick. I pressed him
to my breast and promised that one day, we'd be united forever.

People who don't live here won't understand why my aunt didn't
step in to help me. She couldn't because if she went to the authorities about this situation, she'd be reminded that my father held all
the cards. How could I possibly show that I could take care of my
son? Don't forget that in Jamaica, I was a teenage girl wandering
homeless, and the government didn't give a damn.

I played with Alrick and let him clutch my fingers. I peered into
his eyes and whispered, "I'm your mother."

He'd stare at me as I wiped back tears. I hoped he understood.

"I'm so sorry for leaving you." I'd be missing so much as he was
growing up. His first steps. His first words. Who would he say
"Mama," to?

Paul gestured that I hand Alrick back to him. "We have to get
home."

Reluctantly, I gave up my son, and as I did so it was like tearing
a piece of my heart. Ruefully, I watched Paul bundle up Alrick and
step out the door. I saw them fade down the street, and that tear
in my heart ripped open a little more with loneliness and despair.

I returned to the streets and stayed with friends, where I was offered a meal or a place to stay. But not always. Sometimes, I'd have to sleep in the woods like a stray animal.

A few days later I found myself in Brighton where I chatted up a friendship with two girls my age, Doris and Chanel. A sudden rain had sent us darting for cover under an awning outside a market. I could tell they were runaways like me. Somehow, we girls in similar circumstances could spot one another.

When the rain stopped, Doris asked me, "You want to stay with us?"

I replied sure and followed them several blocks to a storefront office. Doris explained the place was a recording studio, and that the owner let them stay for free. Faded posters of musical acts were taped across the front windows and the door. She pulled a key from her pocket and unlocked the entrance. We stepped into an office with plastic chairs facing a desk, papers piled on top, a table, and metal filing cabinets. Framed photographs of musicians hung on the walls. In many of the pictures, the musicians crowded around a nice-looking guy with a beard.

"That's Jerry," Chanel said. "The owner."

Another door led to narrow room with a long panel crowded with switches and dials.

"That's what they call a mixing board," Doris said.

Through a wall-to-wall window we could observe another room, lined with cork panels. Microphones rested on stands. I had never thought about how music was made, and this place with all its electronic gadgets felt both technical and magical.

Two office chairs on wheels sat on the carpet of the mixing room. I rested in one and reached for the mixing panel.

"Don't touch," Chanel warned. "If Jerry thinks we've messed with his equipment, we're back on the streets."

"Oh, sorry," I said, meekly.

We picked through a stack of CDs. Many appeared locally produced. She loaded one into a CD player in the corner. Soon, the voice of someone covering Marvin Gaye filled the room. We sang along and took turns spinning on the chairs, giggling like we were in an amusement park. The front door opened. Doris stopped the music.

The man who entered was Jerry. He lifted an eyebrow upon noticing me. Doris explained who I was and though Jerry was cordial, he didn't seem interested. He set a briefcase on his desk and began shuffling papers and making phone calls.

We three girls stayed quiet and out of his way. After a while we lay on the floor and napped out of boredom. What woke us was the front door locking behind Jerry.

My stomach growled. I hadn't eaten since morning and it was now late in the afternoon. I gazed about the office. "Does Jerry keep any food around?"

Doris shook her head. "We're on our own."

"Let's go," Chanel said, mysteriously.

I followed her and Doris outside. The air had cooled and the setting sun dragged long shadows across the street. Cars darted around us.

Doris slowed her step to study me. "You look strong."

That was an odd compliment. "I am. Why?"

"Are you afraid of hitting someone?"

"Are we getting into a fight?"

Chanel answered, "We're going find a guy and rob him."

It was my turn to study them. Doris was slight and Chanel was about my height and weight. I couldn't picture them brawling with men.

"Are you in?" Doris asked.

"A particular guy or just somebody off the street?" I replied.

"It can be anybody. Just as long as he's by himself and he looks like he's got money."

The idea intrigued me. I was still stewing with hatred for men, starting with my dad and the way he chased me from my home and my son. Then there was Mark, Alrick's father, for getting me pregnant and then walking away from his responsibilities. Plus Damien and all the other men who had hurt me and tried to take advantage of me. Robbing a man, any man, seemed like a great way to get revenge on behalf of all women.

"Yeah," I said.

We continued down the block to a street teeming with music and neon signs advertising beer and nightclubs. Before, Doris and Chanel had been unassuming teenage girls, and now they sized up the people around us like wolves singling out prey from a flock.

Doris halted. "There's one." She pointed to a man leaning against a lamppost. He lit a cigarette and puffed on it languidly. He was dressed well enough and wore a nice watch so that meant he probably had some cash on him. And he looked a bit drunk.

"There's an alley down the street," Doris said. "I'll take him there."

I guess she meant that's where we would mug him. Chanel and I let Doris take the lead while we hung back a few steps.

"Hey mister," Doris approached the man, "what are you after this fine evening?"

He gave her a prolonged once-over, smiled, and when he pushed away from the lamppost, I knew he had taken Doris' bait. "I'm after a good time."

"Seems like you've started already."

"Certainly," his face illuminated with desire, "but now that you're here, the best part of the night is ahead of both of us."

I grimaced in disgust. Surely this man knew Doris was too young for him. Perhaps that was part of the attraction. He tried to put one hand on her shoulder but she pulled away, teasing him. He stepped behind her, wobbling a bit.

Chanel and I trailed behind them. The man was not much taller than me, but on the fat side with gray hair on his temples. I imagined that his wife and family were at home while he was out spending the household cash on liquor and women. I looked forward to giving this fool what he deserved.

As we had planned, Doris led him to the alley.

"Where you taking me, girl?" he asked.

"My place. We're almost there."

They pivoted into the alley. Doris scanned to make sure no one else was watching. She took his hand, glanced back at us, and nodded.

It was if someone had opened the throttle of my heart because it raced full speed. Chanel quickened her step and I kept pace, though I fought to keep from rushing and spoiling our attack.

Doris grabbed his hand and pulled.

He tried wrenching it away. She hung onto it and he stumbled backwards, unsteady.

At the moment he started to utter a protest, Chanel launched herself and smashed into his shoulders from behind. His legs gave way and he landed face down in the dirt. Before he could respond, I piled on top and pinned his head down.

"Jump on his shoulders!" Doris shouted.

I jammed my knees into his shoulder blades, using my weight to hold him down. He was either stunned or knocked out. Either way, he didn't protest.

Doris shoved her hand into his right-side pants pockets, Chanel into his left. Doris pulled out a few coins and a key ring. Chanel brandished his wallet. She unfolded it and plucked out the bills. Two thousand, four hundred Jamaican dollars. She balled the money in her fist, tossed the wallet, and jumped to her feet. We sprinted from the alley and slowed down to mix with people on the sidewalk.

My heart hadn't quit racing. I wanted to cry out in exhilaration. Robbing the man had been so easy. Men were so stupid when it came to women.

We hustled down the street, taking care not to look back in case the man started yelling for help. The stolen money paid for a nice dinner and some groceries. The next day we robbed a younger man dressed in a business suit, and he had been carrying enough cash to feed us for the next two days.

On the third day, we were in the studio waiting to head out when Jerry arrived. He called us to the office. Standing beside him was a short but dapper man I instantly recognized as Otis Williams, a musician of some fame here in Jamaica. Because of his Asian features, he's known as the "Black Coolie." It was a real treat meeting a local celebrity.

Jerry explained that we girls were keeping an eye on his studio.

"Can you sing?" Otis asked.

"Sure we can sing," we three gushed.

"Then how about some serious work?" he asked. "I need back-up vocals."

He passed out sheet music. We couldn't read the notes but at least we could sing the lyrics. He and Jerry taught us how to work the mikes and make sound checks. We clamped headphones over our ears to practice a few songs. For a brief moment, we felt like professionals and I had the sense that our lives had taken a really good turn.

But our dreams of becoming professional singers were just that, dreams. Truth was, we sounded awful. Jerry could only perform so much magic fixing our off-key voices with his equipment. Still, Otis brought us along to a couple of his gigs. Fortunately, the instruments were loud, and the audience liquored up so no one complained how much we tortured his music.

Our lack of musical skills aside, things were going well enough. One morning I was helping Doris sort through a pile of CDs when I heard the front door open and my mother, of all people, started yelling at Jerry. I rushed to see what she was doing here and why she was hollering.

When my mother saw me, her eyebrows pinched together in disapproval. "What are you doing with the likes of him?" She pointed at Jerry.

I was surprised by her accusation. "Jerry's been treating me okay."

"You, a teenage girl, hanging out with musicians," she scolded.

I didn't understand her problem. Jerry's studio was the safest place I'd been since leaving home. Above all, I was confused. Mother had so much she could be telling me. About Alrick for starters, and instead she'd come all this way to scold me.

"Nobody has been bothering Petergay," Jerry said.

Mother glowered at him. "No one asked you. And shame on you for taking advantage of these young girls."

Doris and Chanel crowded behind me. "We're fine here."

"I didn't come here to argue," Mother replied. "Petergay, you're going to leave this place. Now!"

I had no choice. Mother was one of the few people in the world who really cared about me. Maybe she had heard something about Jerry that I had missed. I gathered my few belongings in a plastic bag and left with her. She wanted me to return home with her, but I couldn't.

We walked to the bus stop where she caught a bus. Once again, I was stranded.

I stayed two nights with Deborah. Her drug-dealer friend Joshua never showed up and so nothing dramatic happened. She spent most of her time stoned on ganja and staring at me like I was an unwanted cat. When she suggested that I meet another friend of hers—the tone of Deborah's voice suggested a male friend, as in sleep with him—I decided it was time to leave.

I ended up back at Deeta's bar, where she introduced me to another circle of go-go dancers. Nicole and Pamela had moved on. I met Barbara and Katrina, who became my new best friends though I still didn't consider dancing with them at Flippers.

When we traveled about, men didn't hesitate in coming on to us, and especially Katrina, the prettiest one. She was petite like a doll, but feisty and foul-mouthed.

Barbara cued me in that she and Katrina liked to lure men into a trap and roll them. I told her this was nothing new for me and that I was totally onboard.

But I know that sooner or later, we could make a mistake. Our victim might have friends. Or he might recognize us and decide on revenge. So when I spotted a long hunting knife at the market, I stole it while Katrina distracted the owner.

The knife soon came in handy when Katrina lured our victim into a vacant house. I was outside standing guard when I heard Barbara jump the man and the three of them scuffled. The ambush should've been lightning fast, but as the scuffling and cursing continued, that told me the robbery had gone bad.

I rushed inside. A stocky man was on his knees, straddling Barbara who lay on her back, and choking her. His pants were gathered at his ankles. Katrina pulled at his shirt while punching his head.

Brandishing the knife, I sprang forward and kicked the man's arm. Cursing from pain, he rolled off Barbara. Katrina tumbled against the floor.

Before the man could react, I lunged at him with the knife. Its shiny blade caught sunlight spilling through the window, and the knife seemed as big as a sword. His eyes fixed on its sharp edge and he scuttled backwards, his pants trailing between his bare feet.

"Cut me and you go to jail," he said, his voice earnest but betraying fright.

"I cut you and you go to the grave." I lunged at him, slashing the space between us with the blade. He flinched and backed away to the wall.

Hand to her throat, Barbara staggered to her feet. Katrina helped her up and they stumbled outside. I kept the knife up and at the ready in case the man decided to chase us. With his pants down, he couldn't do much, but I wasn't going to take any chances.

Once on the street, we hurried out of the neighborhood. I tucked the knife back into my pants. We didn't say much.

Finally, Barbara said, "Thank you, Petergay." Her voice cracked and she massaged her throat. "I was sure he was going to kill me."

My heart pounded with the *what-if* had I stabbed the man. Even if he deserved it, killing a man would bring the law and I was unsettled about spending the rest of my life in prison because of an idiot like him.

We reached the apartment without further incident. The girls cleaned up and I escorted them to Flippers, then went back home, my knife at the ready.

The next day, Barbara disappeared for about an hour. When she reappeared, she pulled a cloth bundle from her tote and opened it on the bed. The bundle contained a small pistol.

"It's a revolver," she explained. She showed me how to swing out the cylinder and remove its six brass cartridges. "These are the bullets." She pushed them back into the cylinder and clicked it closed. Gripping the pistol, she pointed it with both hands and squinted down its top. "This is how you aim it. Just pull the trigger and *Pow!*"

She gave me the revolver. It wasn't much larger than my hand but felt heavy, dangerous. This was the first time I'd been this close to a real gun, let alone held one. It was spotted with rust, the wooden grip cracked. "Where did you get this?"

"A friend of a friend."

I palmed the gun and wrapped my index finger around the trigger. I pointed it at a picture on the wall and then at our reflections in the armoire mirror. No one better mess with us.

The revolver gave us new confidence. No man, no matter how

big, would put up a fight when you poked a gun in his face. We embarked on a robbery spree and divided the loot. Our victims didn't carry much money so my take was never more than a few thousand Jamaican dollars.

I had to make more money and once again decided to dance. I mean, I was robbing people, threatening them with a knife and a gun. Every robbery was me attacking a society that didn't care about me, so why should I care about it?

I screwed up my courage. Barbara lent me a green and gold sequined outfit. At Flippers, I joined the girls in the dressing room and got ready. I gossiped along with them and pretended that I wasn't so nervous I could throw up.

At last it was my turn on stage. Unlike my previous time here, I was determined not to back down and embarrass myself and my friends. How hard could this dancing be compared to robbing and fighting men? All full of false enthusiasm I strutted from behind the curtain, climbed on the platform, and began to writhe to the music.

"Petergay," someone shouted.

I stopped in mid-step, alarms going off in my head as I recognized the voice. I couldn't see past the glare of the spotlights. A man emerged from the illuminated blur.

Otis Williams.

"Petergay," he exclaimed, astonished. "I never thought I'd see you here."

He gestured at my tiny outfit and acted ashamed for the both of us. "Come down off that stage before your mother finds out what you're doing."

# CHAPTER 8

The music for the other go-go dancers blared around me as Otis Williams' gaze hardened with condemnation. Seconds ago, I was filled with tough-girl bravado; now I was as timid as a kitten.

Though I still wore all the pieces of my sequined outfit, I felt completely naked. My hands jerked to cover my breasts, and I bent forward to better hide myself. "Please, please," I mumbled.

He waited for me to explain, but I was too shocked and humiliated to reply. I clattered off the dance platform. He grabbed my shoulder. "Petergay—"

I pulled free and started for the curtain. I had to get away and had no intention of discussing what I was doing. "Wait for me here," I assured him. "Let me change first."

Parting the curtain, I dashed to the changing room. No matter what I tried, or in what direction I turned, it seemed my life kept spiraling toward disaster. My hands trembled so much that I fumbled with my costume, and out of frustration I tore it off. The other girls in the changing room stared at me. I forced a smile to pretend that I was okay, although I wasn't by far.

After taking a deep breath to calm myself, I changed into my street clothes and hurried to the back door. I paused at the threshold to make sure Williams wasn't outside, and seeing that the way was clear, I scurried into the night.

I knew that when I didn't return, Williams would start asking for me and probably run into Barbara and Katrina. Barbara would discover that I had ripped apart her favorite dance outfit, and for that, she'd surely rat me out to him. That prospect eliminated the option of returning to our apartment, because the three of them might be waiting.

So once again, I'm fleeing like a hunted animal. I wiped at tears of rage and despair. *Why was my life so cursed? What have I done to deserve such mistreatment?*

Remembering a cousin, Khani, who lived nearby, I made my way to her home.

Like most of my relatives, she lived in a small, unassuming house. The kitchen light was on and it shined out the front window. She answered my knock on her door.

We hadn't seen each other in a long time, and she expressed genuine surprise with my appearance. Khani was a small woman and older than me by eight years.

"I'm passing through," I said, "and wonder if I could spend the night."

She invited me in. "Your mother told me what's going on with you."

I waited for Khani to add a measure of disapproval, but she didn't. Instead she asked me to sit at her table where she offered a plate of cold chicken and bread. At the sight of the food I realized how hungry I was and so I readily devoured everything she'd set out.

In my purse, I carried the money I'd stolen with Barbara and Katrina from the last guy we had robbed. I pulled out a couple of dollars and laid them on the table. "It's not much, but I do owe you for your troubles."

"That's not necessary," Khani replied, but took the money anyway.

* * *

The next morning, I headed straight for the local bus park where I pondered my next move. I needed a new place to stay and a way to make money. The dilemma was that a ticket and what I intended to spend for dinner would use the last of my funds, but I couldn't stay there. Sooner or later I'd run into Williams again. No doubt he would tell my mother where he had seen me, adding to the growing tension between us. Every day, this web of anguish and torment seemed to wrap tighter and tighter around me.

As I waited at the bus park, a reedy and elegantly dressed woman approached. I caught her studying me. When I turned toward her, she said, "Excuse me, are you looking for work?" Before I could answer, she explained, "I need a housekeeper for my home in Kingston. I pay well."

Just like that, my fortunes had turned. I now had the opportunity to leave this place for a job. We exchanged names; hers was Nadine. I waited for her to ask more about me, as in where was I from, how old was I, and where have I worked? But she didn't, which was fine with me because my past was what I was trying to escape.

Nadine paid the bus fare to Kingston. During the trip, she talked about all kinds of things—the weather, music, local politics—but didn't reveal much about herself. Even so, I liked her and was thankful for her friendship.

Once in Kingston we walked to her house. She lived in a more

69

modern home than what I was used to, and it was large, with two bedrooms. Besides a gas stove and oven, she owned a color television and a telephone. But I noticed that Nadine didn't mention what my chores would be, and we spent the afternoon chatting, drinking Cokes, and watching TV.

When I was in the bathroom I heard her use the telephone. Since it wasn't any of my business what the call was about, I didn't ask. But the way Nadine looked at me after hanging up, I had the suspicion the topic was about me.

In the late afternoon, for my first chore as housekeeper Nadine gave me money and a list of groceries to buy from the local market. No sooner had I walked out the door than I heard her make another phone call. I halted and cocked my ear toward the door but I couldn't make out what was said.

About an hour later I returned with the groceries. Two men waited at her kitchen table. One appeared thin-boned like Nadine and shared her elongated features. The other man was more compact and wore his hair in loose curls. Nadine introduced the first man as her cousin, Michael, and the other as his friend, Collie. I got the impression that both men had just arrived, and I wondered if they had been the ones Nadine had called earlier.

Michael was sitting next to Nadine. She lit a cigarette. The men looked me over the way all men do, and Michael was especially obvious and rude about it. A slight grin of approval curved his lips and then he slipped a hand into his pants pocket. He withdrew several thousand-dollar bills that he laid in a thin, flat stack on the table.

Michael extended a leg beneath the table and pushed out a chair. "Why don't you sit?"

I looked at him, Nadine, Collie, and the way they all regarded me. I considered the money, the three people around the table, and me. "What's going on?"

Michael stood. He was taller than I realized. He stepped around the table toward me.

Nadine kept drawing smoke from her cigarette and avoided eye contact. She said, "Michael is here for you."

"What are you talking about?" I demanded.

When Nadine's gaze took in the money, at once I made the connection. Her idea of housework was to pimp me out to her cousin.

"Girl, why are you making this hard for yourself?" Michael grabbed my arms and shoved me against the wall. I struggled to get free but he was very strong and I could tell he was used to muscling people. If I'd had my hunting knife or the gun, I would've killed him right then.

I glanced at Nadine with pleading eyes. Angry and panicked, I stomped on Michael's foot, hard, but all he did was register a slight grimace before whipping me around and forcing me on the table. I kicked and screamed, but Michael's grip was like iron. His eyes burned with rage and I could tell that inflicting pain was probably his favorite part of sex.

Collie seized Michael's hands and leaned between him and me. "Stop it, Michael. The girl doesn't want to play."

*Play?* Michael was intent on raping me.

His grip loosened, and I jerked free. Collie stepped between us and nudged Michael to keep his distance.

Nostrils flaring, Michael stared at me and I could tell that his blood was boiling. He growled, "What's she to you, Collie?"

"She's just a girl that wants to be left alone. Leave her be. She's not worth the trouble."

Michael pointed to the cash. "Nadine, you and I had a deal."

"I brought you a girl," she answered. "It's not my problem if you can't handle her."

Nadine's comment prompted Michael to lunge past Collie for me. But Collie was ready. He caught Michael in a bear hug, which gave me time to scoot toward the front door.

"Stop!" Michael shouted.

I froze in place.

"You are not to leave until we figure this out." He shrugged out of Collie's grasp.

I didn't see what there was to figure out.

Michael slapped the table to get Nadine's attention. "Petergay is not to leave the house until I decide what to do with her."

Nadine sneered at him.

He gripped her jaw and held her head still so he could glare into her eyes. "If she's gone when I get back, you and I will have business."

Nadine grabbed his wrist and worked her jaw free. "Don't you worry, she'll be here."

Michael whisked the cash off the table, nodded at Collie, and they left.

I saw this as an opportunity to escape and gathered my purse.

Nadine remained alert enough to notice what I was up to. She nodded to the closest bedroom. "Go lie down in there. And don't try leaving. Once Michael finds another girl and gets it out of his system, he'll leave you alone."

I retreated to the bedroom where I spied a nail file on the

dresser. I palmed it to use as a weapon in case Michael came after me again. I lay on the bed. From this angle, I could see into the kitchen and in turn, Nadine could watch me.

I remained as still as possible. Although I thought I was too frightened and nervous to fall asleep, I was so tired that I did doze off. The front door closing and loud chatter from the kitchen awakened me. Michael and Collie had returned. My breath caught and I tightened my grip on the nail file.

Michael stumbled toward the bedroom and halted at the door. I didn't turn my head but observed him out the corners of my eyes. By the way he steadied himself in the doorway I could tell he was either drunk or high. I readied the nail file in case he came after me.

But he didn't. He returned to the kitchen to gossip about something with Nadine and Collie. After a time—a half hour, an hour, I couldn't tell—the kitchen light was turned off and the house grew quiet. When someone entered the bedroom, I braced myself for a fight. But it was Nadine who lay beside me and went to sleep.

\*\*\*

The next day, Nadine put me to work cleaning the house, so I was doing domestic work, only I was doing it for free. I swept and mopped the floors and then scrubbed laundry in a tub. Although Collie had saved me from getting raped by Michael, he remained loyal to him and helped the others keep watch over me. One of them was always minding the front door and another the back door.

Late in the afternoon, some men arrived at the house and my three captors met with them on the front stoop. I saw my chance.

The laundry I'd washed, Nadine had hung on clotheslines behind the house. I needed extra clothes and noticed a set of her pants and a blouse that should fit me. I tiptoed out the back door, snatched those clothes, and sprinted away.

***

I returned to the bus station and caught a bus to St. Elizabeth. It was late when I arrived and I wandered a bit before I ended up at the farmer's market, now closed and deserted. I found my mother's empty stall, crawled beneath the table, and slept the night.

The next morning, I was wakened by the first vendors setting up their wares and had to leave before they accused me of being a thief. I visited a couple of friends and though I got something to eat, no one offered me a place to stay the night.

Since I missed my son, I screwed up my courage enough to venture close to my father's house in the hopes of catching a glimpse of my brother Paul. I wanted to ask him to bring Alrick to me. But I never saw Paul that day.

A couple of blocks from my father's house I ran into Mark, Alrick's father. He acted genuinely pleased to see me.

"Petergay," Mark exclaimed, "how have you been?"

"I'm fine, but how is Alrick?"

"Alrick is doing great. He's growing up so fast."

That news was bittersweet. I was happy that our son was healthy, but sad that I was missing out on being with him.

Mark asked where I was staying and when I admitted I had no place to go, he offered his home—where we'd sleep separately, he on his bed, me on the floor on a comforter.

Very early in the morning, a loud banging on the door woke me with a start. I rose from the floor. A woman was outside, screaming, "Mark, I know that whore is inside with you!"

Mark jumped out of bed. "It's Josie, my girlfriend."

The moment he opened the door, Josie tried to charge past him. She wielded a large butcher knife and repeatedly stabbed it into the door while yelling, "Petergay! Petergay! Sleep with my man, will you! I'll cut you to pieces."

"No, it's not like that," I protested, though I could see that Josie was firmly set on attacking me.

She kicked and pushed against the door, screaming loud enough to wake the neighborhood. Mark leaned into the door and hollered over his shoulder, "Petergay, go out the back!"

With the crazy woman out front, I didn't need to be told twice. I grabbed my things and rushed out the back door, Josie screaming, "I'll get you! There's no place that you can hide."

I ran for several blocks and then rested beneath a tree. I was too keyed up to sleep again and remained awake until dawn. Again, no matter what I did, people would twist circumstances to fault me. If I could, I'd take my son and run away from the island to start over. But I couldn't, so the best I could do was make it through another day.

I needed to find a more-or-less permanent place to stay. Since the time I was first on my own, my favorite accommodation had been the recording studio. I made my way back there but Jerry didn't look pleased to see me again.

"I had to kick your friends, Chanel and Doris, out," he said. "They were causing trouble."

"That's all right. We weren't that close, anyway."

"If you're expecting to stay here, forget it. Otis won't allow it."

"Why's that?"

"He didn't say, he just took off for Kingston. But he did instruct me that if you showed up again, he wanted to talk to you."

Probably to scold me, which I didn't need.

With nowhere else to go, I hung around the bus station to see what opportunities developed. Though my situation remained uncertain, I was remarkably steady. At least I was alive and whole. I shuddered as I thought what I'd look like if Josie had carved me up with her big knife.

I passed a large man leaning against a taxi, which was parked in the shadow of a big, leafy tree. Eying me, he asked, "Where are you going this fine day?"

Most times when a man offered a comment, it was a come-on. But his friendly tone invited me to linger, especially as I had nothing else to do.

"Nowhere," I answered.

"Get out of the sun." He waved that I should join him in the shade. He offered one immense hand, which I shook, and we exchanged names. His was Steve, and he added, "On the street I'm known as Fisher."

Scars wrinkled his broad face. More scars covered his hands and thick forearms. Even though Fisher was a rough-looking character, I could tell he was a good-hearted man.

"Do you live around here, Petergay?"

Embarrassed that I was homeless, I pointed in the direction of my father's home. "I live that way."

A man carrying a suitcase approached from the direction of the bus station. "Taxi," he called out.

Fisher pushed away from his car. "You need anything, Petergay, come by here."

For the next two days, I roamed the streets and slept either in the woods or in empty houses. When strange men followed me, I returned to the bus park and said hello to Fisher. The sight of his gnarled face was enough to scare anyone away. Besides his protective nature, what I also liked about him was that he didn't pry into my business.

One early afternoon, Fisher said he had a friend he'd like me to meet.

"What kind of a friend?" I thought back to my experience with Nadine and Michael.

"A nice guy. From America. He's here on vacation and I'm showing him around Jamaica."

I'd never met anyone from America before. So far, Fisher hadn't done anything to betray my trust so I answered, "Sure, why not?"

"Good," Fisher replied. "I have to run fares so meet me back here at five. We'll go then."

I walked off in search of relatives I might get a meal from. At the appointed time, I returned to the park. Fisher drove me in his cab for a long way until we ended up at a bar close to the beach. There were plenty of people around so I didn't feel isolated or threatened.

Inside the bar, Fisher led me to the only white man in the place. He was sitting at a back table, sipping beer. He looked in his late forties and wore a beard. When he saw us approaching, he locked eyes on me and rose to his feet. This was the first time in my life anyone had stood to greet me, and I was surprised and impressed by the gesture. First, he said hello to Fisher and then extended his hand toward me.

"Allen Harper," he said. "It's a pleasure."

Allen's sincere politeness left me speechless. We shook hands. His grip was soft, like his expression. Everything about him was soft, and I could tell his life wasn't one of hard physical labor.

As we sat, his gaze stayed on my face. He didn't ogle me. He was the first white person I'd ever talked with and he treated me with warm respect.

"Fisher has told me a lot about you," Allen said. "He says you're a remarkable young woman."

*In what way?* I wanted to ask. There was a lot of mystery about Allen, and it brought questions that needed answers.

He added, "I'd like to get to know you better but I leave tomorrow to return home. My visa has expired."

"Where is your home?"

"Washington."

I couldn't picture what that place looked like. When I thought of America I imagined what I'd seen on television—New York City, Los Angeles, and California beaches, and that's about it.

He pulled a small memo pad from his pocket and scribbled his name and telephone number on a page that he tore free. "I won't be back for at least two months. If you should need me for anything, don't hesitate to call and I'll do my best to help."

"Help in what?"

Allen shrugged. "I don't know. But it's always good to know someone who can help."

# CHAPTER 9

Allen and I didn't talk much. Truth was, the meeting was uncomfortable. This white guy I'd never met before was shining on to me. However, with Fisher there, I didn't feel threatened. Allen's attention wasn't creepy, only uncertain, and so I didn't know where this situation was headed.

Fisher offered relief from the awkwardness when he said, "I have to get back to the bus station."

Since he was my ride, I had to go as well. I slipped Allen's note into my pocket. Allen reached toward me, and I took his hand.

"We'll see each other soon," he assured me.

Evidently, he was aware of circumstances concerning me that I didn't know about. But he had been charming in an odd white-guy way, so I smiled and nodded.

On the drive back to St. Elizabeth, I asked, "Fisher, how well do you know Allen?"

"Well enough, I suppose."

"What does he want from me?"

"Like he said. To know you better."

"But why?" To all but a few close relatives and friends, I was a disposable acquaintance so I couldn't fathom why a stranger had this interest in me.

Fisher shrugged. "When he returns to Jamaica, you can ask him then."

"And when is he returning to Jamaica?"

Fisher shrugged again.

I tucked the mystery about Allen into a recess of my mind and concerned myself with getting by on the streets of town. Once back in St. Elizabeth, my life returned to its routine, a routine that had become a rut I'd fallen into during the three years since my father chased me from home.

*Three years!* Three years of living like a stray dog, begging for scraps. Three years of wandering from place to place, seeking shelter from the rain and from brutes who would harm me. Three years of standing on the sidelines while my son Alrick grew up without me. He'd learned to walk, learned to talk, had been potty-trained with someone else teaching him. I made the opportunity to see him when I could and nurtured my promise to him that one day I'd return and claim him forever.

Now three years down this road and that day seemed as far away from becoming a reality as the moment I'd made that promise. Sometimes I fell into a funk about how I was fooling myself that my situation would get better.

Then I spotted a tiny weed that grew through a crack in the sidewalk. The pavement had heaved around the plant, and so it was obvious that the weed had pushed through and broken the pavement.

Its seed had germinated with nothing to sustain it but the will to exist. That ordinary weed had slowly but relentlessly fractured four inches of solid concrete. If this simple plant had prevailed against such formidable resistance, why couldn't I?

I made it through my days by getting meals from family or friends, and a place to spend the night if I could manage. Fisher provided an emotional refuge and I was waiting at the bus park to meet him when I heard, "Petergay, is that you?"

It was Fabian, an older friend who I hadn't seen in a long time as he lived in Westmoreland. "What brings you to these parts?" he continued. "Shouldn't you be in school?"

After overcoming my surprise at seeing him I replied, "I'm looking for work," while ignoring his question about why I wasn't in school.

"Where are you staying?" he asked.

"No place. I just got here," I lied as I didn't want to explain that I was homeless.

Fabian walked from the bus park and motioned that I tag along. "Come stay with my family. You can look for work in Westmoreland."

Regretfully, I wanted to say goodbye to Fisher since I didn't know when I'd see him again and I feared that he would worry about me for no reason.

Fabian had long, lanky legs that paced rapidly over the ground. We met with his friend and piled into a little car for the ride to Fabian's house. Once there, his mother greeted me warmly.

After dinner, to show my appreciation for the hospitality, I cleaned up the dishes, and while I stayed at their home I swept and dusted the rooms or helped in the kitchen.

A couple of days later, Fabian returned from a morning errand to announce, "Great news, Petergay. I've found you a good job."

This was great news, and I appreciated that he was looking out for me.

"I talked to some friends at the golf club," he explained, "and they need caddies. Is this something you're willing to do?"

"Of course, but I don't know anything about golf."

"They'll teach you. You get a uniform and paid training."

I couldn't believe my good luck. Things were finally turning for the better.

Fabian added that my first day wouldn't start for two weeks. In the meantime, and as much as I enjoyed his mother's company, I had to hang out with girls my age. I met a few of the locals and the two that I got close to were Sandra and her friend, Shernet Fowler, who was known as Marcia. We tended to spend time in the caddy shack.

Marcia acted especially curious about me. "What brings you to Westmoreland?"

"Work," I replied as though I had come here deliberately for a job rather than drifted in. "I've found a job at the golf course."

"What else have you done?"

I told them I had been a back-up singer for Otis Williams. "But it didn't last long." Since I'd been on the streets, the only other real job I'd had was my brief tenure at Flippers. I felt at ease around Sandra and Marcia and so opened up to them. "I was a go-go dancer."

Sandra raised her eyebrows and winced in disgust. "How could you such a thing? It's bad enough men feel free to stare and touch us like we're public property, but to show yourself off like that?"

I was too embarrassed by my experience to explain that I hadn't danced naked. Too many people in my life judged me without bothering to help.

Marcia put her hand on my arm in a protective gesture. "Sandra, stop it. We know how hard it is for us women here."

I didn't have to justify myself to anyone, even Marcia, but her defense of me and her understanding of my past made me like her more.

As we were unaccompanied young women, men tended to circle us like sharks. Of course, we couldn't help but notice their stares and leers. I would glower at these men, and my harsh looks would ward them away from me. But then they focused their attentions on Sandra and Marcia.

One evening, at the nearby park, one fellow swatted Marcia's bottom. I immediately jumped in front of him. "Who gave you permission to do that?"

He reeled in surprise that he'd been caught, and that it was a woman my age calling him out on it.

He gave an oily smile. "Your friend should be grateful."

My hands clenched to punch him, and I unloaded a string of curses. I didn't know what was going to happen, but if we fought, it would be like he was grappling with a wildcat. He was lucky I wasn't packing a weapon.

His friends teased, "What kind of a man you are? Fighting a girl?"

He stepped back, hands open and raised. "No, no. I'm not going to fight her. She's just a little hot-headed."

But I wasn't going to let this go. Marcia tugged my arm. My gaze stayed pinned on the man. He was just like the others, a boor, an oaf, a loser who thought we women existed only for his entertainment. I had no patience for him or his kind. If I had to, I'd brawl with all of them; I wasn't afraid.

That afternoon, when I returned to Fabian's, my brother Paul was waiting for me, his expression heavy with distress. "Petergay, you need to come home at once."

"What's going on?"

"It's Alrick. He has died."

I paused, thinking I had not heard right. Paul's face remained grim. I didn't want to believe what he said, but as the word "died" dragged through my mind, it pulled my world down with it. My legs turned to rubber, and it was only through a mighty effort on my part that I didn't crumple to the ground. "Tell me everything. What did he die from?"

"An accident."

I knew well enough what this meant. In Jamaica, when someone died from an "accident," that was code for that they had succumbed from something else. But what could've have killed my son?

Paul said, "Father says you can come home now." Had it taken the death of my son for my father to at last welcome me?

I was lost in a haze of anguish, unable to comprehend what to do next. Paul led me to the car he had borrowed for the trip. We both kept quiet as the enormity of the tragedy smothered any attempt at conversation. I stewed in my grief and broke down, sobbing the entire ride home.

The promise I had made to my son was now in tatters. I'd had three years to get him but allowed the time to sift through my fingers like sand, and this realization added guilt to my sorrow.

When we arrived at my father's house, I saw that he commiserated outside, in the shadow of a tree by the corner of the house. He stared at the ground, stoop-shouldered, as if struggling to bear the weight of his loss.

"Mother is inside," Paul said.

"Where is Alrick?"

"With the authorities. Mother can tell you what happened."

I got out of the car and called to my father. When he noticed me, his face withered in sadness and unexpected compassion. I staggered inside the house and found Mother on her bed. The light was off, the curtains drawn, and the bedroom was as murky as a crypt. At this time of the day, my mother was usually a tornado of activity, putting away laundry or fixing dinner. Now it was like Alrick's death had gnawed a hole in her soul through which her life's energy seeped out. She stared at the ceiling, her eyes pooled with tears. I eased onto the bed beside her.

I told myself to be strong, but the sight of Alrick's clothes in the room tore my resolve apart. Mother clasped my hand and began to cry. Drawn into her sorrow, I folded myself over her and joined in her lamentations. We wailed and sobbed. It was a day when all the tears in the world were not enough to wash away our ache.

Eventually, we wrung ourselves dry of tears. Looking at me through eyes bruised with pain, Mother brought my hand to her cheek. "Petergay," she whispered, "I have to tell you the truth about what happened to Alrick."

I had calmed down enough to take in the news, in whatever form it was delivered.

"A sickness was going around the neighborhood," Mother explained. "Do you remember Angelica Lindsay, the woman down the street?"

I vaguely recalled her and nodded.

"Her son was stricken with a virus and died, too."

"Virus?" I shuddered as I imagined our air teeming with dangerous germs. How could we defend ourselves against that? "Why didn't you go to the doctor?"

"I did but not right away. No one told us there was a virus. When the fever hit Alrick, I did what we have always done. I bundled him to sweat the fever out." Mother began sobbing again. "But during the second night of his sickness, his temperature was getting worse so I knew something was very wrong. Early the next morning I rushed him to the clinic. But as the doctor hadn't arrived, the staff said there was nothing they could do so I had to wait outside on the stoop. And it was there that Alrick died in my arms."

I hung my head in despair. Mother had only done what I would have in her situation, for we didn't know any better.

She said, "When the doctor finally arrived, he took a quick look at Alrick, pronounced him dead, and seeing as there was nothing the clinic could do for him, told me to take him to the police station across the street."

"What now?"

"We do the business of giving him a proper burial. But since he is your son, you alone can claim him."

Mother and I collected Alrick's birth certificate and made our way to the police station. It had been years since I'd walked so openly in this neighborhood, and people stared. But I didn't care. A piece of my heart had been amputated, and it was a wound that would never heal.

At the station, the cop on duty watched us enter and approach his desk. He could tell that we'd been crying and were under great emotional strain, but he regarded us with official indifference. He knitted his fingers over his desk blotter and waited for us to begin.

"I was here this morning," Mother explained. "I left my grandson. He passed away from the virus."

The cop didn't respond other than to ask, "And why have you returned?"

"I have to claim him," I replied.

The cop cocked an eyebrow at me. "Who are you?"

"I am his mother." I placed the birth certificate on the desk and unfolded it.

The cop only glanced at the form. "What's his name?"

"Alrick Stewart."

He pointed at Mother. "Your name?"

"Sadie Dunkley."

The cop flipped through a ledger and slid a fingertip down the entries until he stopped at one. "Wait here." He got up from behind his desk and headed down a hall toward the back of the station. Mother and I took seats in the plastic chairs by the front door and waited.

I could never have imagined such a terrible fate for Alrick and me. The rapping of knuckles on the wall called my attention. It was the desk cop. "Your son is at the hospital morgue." He gave us directions.

At the hospital we were introduced to the coroner, a slightly older man. He ushered us into the morgue and toward a steel table in the middle of the room. The chilled air carried the odor of rancid meat.

A medical technician brought a small object swaddled in a towel. He wore a surgical mask and yellow rubber gloves as if to not contaminate himself with what was in the bundle.

I held still but my insides swirled with dread. How did one prepare herself to see her dead child?

The technician unfurled the towel as he dropped the object. It was Alrick. His small naked body thumped rigidly on the table like a frozen chicken.

The casual disregard the hospital staff had for him, and Mother, and me, shocked me with its brutal apathy.

"Is this your boy?" the coroner asked, smirking as if my reclaiming this corpse was the punch line of a cruel joke.

I stared at the stiff body of my son. But the sight of him stirred something unexpected. The sorrow that had so crippled me gave way to a flood of anger. Though my precious Alrick was the world to me, he was nothing to the people here.

My tiny son had been more than the victim of a virus, he was also the victim of our poverty, and our powerlessness, and of a bureaucracy that only barely concerned itself with our welfare. This was more than the story of my son's death, for it was another example of what it was like to be poor and neglected in Jamaica.

At that instant, I made myself another promise, one that I knew I would keep.

When the time comes, I will never treat another human being the way these cops had treated Alrick and me.

# CHAPTER 10

We buried Alrick on Sunday. People gathered at the cemetery in their best church clothes. For these brief, dark hours my father and I engaged in a truce. We set aside our animosity to share our remorse over my son's death.

When you lose someone as precious as a child, there seems endless depth to the sorrow. When Alrick's casket was lowered into the grave, I had to hold steady to keep from throwing myself after him. Though I knew it wasn't possible, I wanted to be with him forever.

After the funeral, I continued to grieve until I was an empty husk, unable to wring one more tear. When I was at rock bottom, I realized that nothing would bring back my little one. The best thing I could do as a tribute to Alrick was to live as well as I could.

The following Monday I showed up at the Negril Hills Golf Club to begin my training as a caddy. I changed into my uniform and gave everyone smiles to show that I was a pleasant and eager employee. But at every break I'd lock myself in the bathroom, lose my composure, and crumple in grief. Try as I might, I couldn't shake the sadness and guilt over losing my son.

After several minutes of crying, I'd look in the mirror and scold myself. *Get it together, Petergay. You're risking this job, this great opportunity. Remember your promise to yourself. If for nothing else, do it for your son.*

I'd wash my face, take a moment to put on my happiest expression, and then join the others. Alrick's passing was certainly known in the club but no one made mention of it or asked why I spent so much time in the bathroom.

After my training, I was assigned to the roster of caddies and put to work. It was a fun, low-stress job where I spent a lot of time outdoors on the beautiful grounds. A few weeks into my tenure, I was assigned to a white couple, Gene and Aznina Czaplinsky, visiting from the U.S. They took a shine to me and after several visits to the course, Aznina asked, "Petergay, my husband and I want to attend a Bob Marley concert, and we need a babysitter. Are you free to look after our son?"

It was extra money and since the couple had been so nice to me, I readily agreed. They were staying in Negril and while at their hotel I attended to their baby, fascinated by his features. I didn't have much experience with white people and especially with a white baby. What intrigued me were his pale eyes and his hair, so fine and light-colored, unlike the dense black hair of a Jamaican baby. Playing with this little white boy made me miss my Alrick, but the way this baby reacted to me with smiles and giggles made me feel better about myself. The last time I was with the Czaplinskis, Aznina gave me her home phone number from the U.S. "Just in case," she explained.

On my days off from the golf course I returned to St. Elizabeth and met up with Fisher to reassure him that I was okay. We were sipping Cokes in the shade by his taxi stand when he abruptly said, "Allen is back in Jamaica."

Shocked, I stared at Fisher. I'd completely forgotten about Allen. "Why are you telling me this?"

"Because he wants to meet you. Remember he told you that?"

That first time I had been with Allen was a strange experience and I came away from it not certain about his intentions. Since then, just as I'd forgotten about him, I was convinced he had forgotten about me.

Fisher said, "Allen says he has a plan to help you."

"Help me in what way? I have a good job. Things look like they're finally turning around. I don't need his help."

Fisher shrugged, and his enormous shoulders flexed around his big neck. "I don't know how he intends to help you. But it wouldn't hurt to see him, would it?"

I looked at the situation from all angles. No, I couldn't see a reason not to meet him. "All right." I scribbled the number for the golf course clubhouse and told Fisher to contact me there.

Fisher nodded. "Very good. I'll let him know."

"And then?" I asked.

Fisher smiled. "We'll see."

\*\*\*

Fisher came to Hatfield where I lived, to pick me up to see Allen. It was Fisher calling. "Petergay, I hope you have an appetite. Allen wants to meet you tonight at a restaurant in Mandeville. Can you make it?"

"Yes," I blurted, even though it felt like events regarding Allen were moving too fast.

"I can pick you up," Fisher offered.

"No, no. It's too far out of your way. Tell me the name of the restaurant and I'll make my way there."

"What I do on my own time is my business," he answered. "It won't be a bother."

\*\*\*

On the drive to the restaurant Fisher chatted about a lot of things, except Allen. For the meeting, I had changed out of my caddy uniform and into a nice blue dress. Though I had no idea what Allen had in mind, I wanted to look my best.

At the restaurant, Fisher let me out so that I could proceed inside alone. I spotted Allen right away. He was at a side table and casually dressed like a typical, well-heeled American tourist. His bearded Caucasian face brightened when he saw me. He was the only person in my life who reacted this way to me, which left me both flattered and wary.

When I drew close, he stood and took my hand. His was soft and warm and also a bit clammy like he was nervous. "Petergay, I've missed you so much. Since I've left, all I could think about was coming back for you."

"Allen, I missed you too," I lied, saying this because the truth would ruin the moment.

"I have a way to help you," he said.

Like I had explained to Fisher, I didn't see how Allen could help me.

He hadn't let go of my hand and he stepped away from his chair to sink to one knee. He took my hand in both of his and gazed adoringly into my eyes. "Petergay, will you marry me?"

The question stupefied me. The gears in my mind accelerated to maximum speed as I processed his words.

"Marry me," he continued, "and your life will change for the better. You will no longer have to struggle to make ends meet because I'll take care of you."

What was he saying? I'd always thought that you married someone because you were in love. I hardly knew Allen and he hardly knew me—where did this notion of marriage come from? We had only met once before and barely talked enough for him to make a deep impression on me.

On the other hand, all my life I was like dust under other people's feet, and for the first time someone acted like they truly desired me. I was still trying to find words to express my confusion when I heard myself say, "Yes, of course I'll marry you."

Allen's face widened into an incandescent smile. In that moment, I was overcome with a joy I'd never before felt. It was like all the shackles holding me broke loose and I was open to all of life's possibilities.

Allen pushed himself upright. Letting go of my hand, he reached into his trouser pocket and produced a paperclip pinched around several twenty- and fifty-dollar bills, American. He thrust the money into my hand. "I know how you Jamaicans like to take care of your family. Share your good fortune with them."

I didn't count the cash but guessed it was more than five hundred dollars. When I had been kicked out of my home, I had promised myself that one day I'd return flush with money to prove that I could do all right on my own. Had that day arrived?

I regarded Allen in a new light. All suspicions and reservations about him disappeared and I saw him as someone I thought I'd never see, my knight in shining armor.

Allen pushed back a chair and offered it to me. "Let's celebrate with dinner."

***

During that dinner we set a date to get married, and it was to be a simple civic wedding. Allen and I talked through the night. He would return to the U.S. and apply for a spousal visa. Once that was approved, I'd fly to his home in Olympia, Washington—wherever that was. Everything that he told me about America sounded so exotic and promising.

Fisher returned to give me a ride back to Hatfield, and I left light-headed about the prospects of my new future.

The next morning, I visited an appliance store and ordered a gas stove to be delivered to my mother's house. I made it a point to be there when the stove arrived. With the delivery truck rumbling outside her door, I rushed inside. Fortunately, my father wasn't home. Mother was in the kitchen, cutting vegetables when I stepped in.

"Mother," I exclaimed, "I have a big surprise for you."

She set the knife down and wiped both hands on her apron. Her look of amusement would surely vanish when she saw the stove.

I directed one of the deliverymen to her old wood-burning stove. "That has to go."

"Petergay," Mother asked, dumbfounded, "what are you doing?"

Fortunately, her stove hadn't been used recently so it was cool enough for the deliveryman to carry outside. Mother stood by the door, open-mouthed as she watched the deliveryman and his assistant bring in the gas stove. Besides its four burners and oven, this new stove used odorless natural gas that eliminated the kerosene smell. They set it where the kerosene stove had been and began connecting the new stove to a tank of gas outside.

Mother kept prodding me how I had managed to buy the stove, but I distracted her by talking about its features. I knew our conversation about Allen was going to be uncomfortable. Discussing him over tea brewed on Mother's brand-new stove should put her in a more receptive mood. Neighbors popped in to regard the new appliance and Mother graciously complimented me for being such a thoughtful daughter.

When the tea was ready we sat on the bed. My reluctance at discussing the circumstances about the stove had greatly aroused her curiosity. She sipped her tea and waited for me. Where to begin?

With Allen, naturally. Mother stayed quiet for several minutes and finally spoke when I said that I had agreed to marry him.

"You hardly know the man," she said. "How can you justify running off and marrying such a stranger?"

I hadn't come to grips with an answer that satisfied me, other than after so much had gone wrong in my life, marrying Allen felt like the right thing to do.

"And a white man from America, no less?" she pressed.

"It's a big change, for sure," was the only reply I could muster.

"Will you be leaving us?"

I held her hand. "I won't be leaving you, I'll be leaving the island, that's all. I'll send money home."

Mother snorted. "Don't let having money blind you to the duties and burden of being a wife. Marriage is difficult work and

95

the disagreements between you and your husband will be hard to weather if you don't love one another." She squeezed my hand. "Do you love him?"

Considering that I was going to marry Allen and move away with him, my answer could only be, "Yes."

My brief answer seemed to have satisfied her somewhat. "Will you have children?"

I hadn't thought about that. "Not right away. Let me get settled first."

"There's something else," Mother said. "Tongues around here will wag, a black girl like you running off with a white American."

"I'm not running off," I corrected. "I'm getting married."

"Folks won't make the distinction. A black girl getting involved with a white man, an older white man, means she thinks she's too good for her kind—"

"That's not true," I interrupted. "What would you prefer that I do? Up until now my life hasn't been a picnic. But at least I have something to show for my efforts." I glanced toward her new stove.

She smiled to acknowledge my gift. "Petergay, if I had the answer to all of life's big questions I'd be a very rich woman. But I don't. What I can tell you is to proceed with your eyes wide open."

\*\*\*

While Mother's acknowledgment of my marriage to Allen wasn't exactly an enthusiastic blessing, she did admit the possible benefits, one of which was I'd be going to America—the land of opportunity—and leaving my problems behind in Jamaica. I considered myself fortunate with my job at the golf course since it provided income in an environment where I met people outside my usual crowd. That put me out of earshot of malicious gossip.

One afternoon I was caddying for a woman named Angela. I could tell from her accent that she was from the U.S. and since I would eventually be going there, I decided to chat her up.

"Where in America do you live?" I asked.

"New York."

I tried to picture the place from what I'd seen on television. "What work do you do?"

"I'm a registered nurse," she replied.

Another reason that I struck up this conversation was that she was one of those warm and agreeable people who are a delight to be around. And now she was the first nurse I'd ever had more than a brief conversation with. Our talk made me entertain the idea of becoming a nurse. I didn't know how I'd do it or when, but the idea had been planted in my mind.

\*\*\*

Allen and I got quietly married and we moved into a small apartment in Mandeville. He and I were getting along well, and I hadn't been so happy since my carefree days of childhood.

But as with most things in life, every bright ray of sunshine casts a shadow. The shadow in this case was when my friend Phillipa called the apartment to tell me that Officer Brown, who was a family friend as well as a policeman, had dropped by her house. He brought information about Allen—Brown preferred to give us the details in person—and he would return to her house that evening.

Phillipa was beside herself with apprehension about Allen. We were having tea when a car halted outside her kitchen. Officer Brown then appeared at her door. Entering, he took his cap off and twirled it nervously in his hands. Though he smiled as we exchanged greetings, I could tell he had unfortunate information to share.

At last, Brown revealed his message. "We arrested your husband Allen in Kingston. He was smoking crack."

The news stunned me. "What? Where is he?"

"When we learned he was your husband, we let him go without pressing charges. The only drugs he had on his person was the crack cocaine in the pipe. But in asking people who know him, we learned that his true business in Jamaica is getting high as often as possible. He has problems."

This revelation was a gut punch. My knight in shining armor was in reality a dope fiend. I turned to Mother for advice and half expected her to give me an I-told-you-so look. But she didn't, and that let me know I was on my own as far as Allen was concerned.

"What happens now?" I asked.

"Though we didn't charge him," Brown replied, "he's violated the conditions of his visa. He has to leave soon, either on his own or he gets deported."

My world became a maelstrom of emotions: hurt, anger, bitterness, resentment, helplessness.

Nervous and uncomfortable, Officer Brown shuffled his feet. "That is all I know. If anything changes, I'll send word or stop by." He put his cap back on and left. His car cranked over and motored away.

As you churn through life's experiences, you think you have everything figured out, or that you've learned enough so that nothing trips you up. But Allen smoking crack was a betrayal that dropped me flat on my face. I didn't have much to be proud of from my time on the streets, but I could hold my head up over the fact that I stayed away from drugs. Whatever problems you had, they only got worse if you indulged. I had yet to meet one person whose life improved because of drug abuse. And now, irony of ironies, my husband, the man who I committed my life to, had a drug habit.

I had asked Allen to pick me up from Phillipa's house. My plan was that I would have learned from Officer Brown what concerned Allen, and we could've discussed the situation while it was fresh in my mind. Little did I suspect such deceit.

Allen arrived about a half hour after Brown had left. My husband brought a sack of groceries and carried himself innocently as if he hadn't been recently arrested for drugs.

No sooner had he placed the groceries on the table than Phillipa blew up.

"What kind of a man are you?" she exclaimed. "Making all kinds of promises to my friend, then go off with your crackhead bums to smoke drugs? How dare you disgrace the Dunkley name!"

Allen shrunk from her like a timid cat. With every moment, Phillipa's fury only intensified. But her accusations about his character spilled over to me, since by marrying him, I had been blind to his flaws. At one point, I expected her to grab a frying pan and beat him over the head, and maybe mine as well.

Allen's eyes sagged and he had all the bearing of a whipped child. He kept repeating, "I'm sorry. I'm sorry," his voice soft as a whimper. Had he not brought this shame on himself, I would've felt sorry for him.

When Phillipa was at last done, she vented the last of her fury at me. "He's yours now. It's your job to keep him in line."

Allen tipped his head to the door, our cue to leave. On my way out I was tempted to grab the frying pan and bust his head.

\*\*\*

That night I made Allen sleep someplace other than our bed. I lay awake, my thoughts storming with how I'd been deceived about Allen and how I was to proceed from here. The big problem was that we were married, which wasn't an easy process to undo.

The next morning he departed our apartment early, explaining that he had to make arrangements to leave Jamaica. I left for work, and while I was gone I wouldn't have been surprised if he had been picked up again. I know how these crack-heads are.

When I returned to the apartment Allen showed me his airline ticket. He'd be flying away in two days. "Nothing's changed between us," he said. "I made a mistake. I should've been honest about my past and my problems with drugs. But all that is behind me, baby. When we get to Olympia, you'll see how good things can get."

I had to believe him. Wheels were in motion and I had no option but to see our plans through.

"As soon as I get home I'll apply for the spousal visa," he added. "Be patient. The process will take months. I'll keep in touch by telephone."

The day he boarded the flight to the U.S., I was overcome by a profound melancholia. Doubts circled in my head. What if Allen changed his mind about us? What if he got picked up for drugs back at his home? What if there were problems with the visa?

Since neither Mother nor I had a telephone, Allen would call a neighbor and schedule a time that I'd be there to accept his call. I didn't dare do this business using the clubhouse phone. Despite the reasons for his early departure from Jamaica, when he did call I loved hearing his voice. It let me know that our plans for the future weren't a delusion.

After four long months, I finally got the news. "Petergay," he said happily, "your visa was approved. I'll be sending you the documents and money for your airline tickets."

On November 7, 1998, at 6:05 AM, I boarded an American Airlines jet in Montego Bay. I would be leaving Jamaica for the first time in my life. I was leaving much behind, but there was much to look forward to.

# CHAPTER 11

During the flight from Jamaica to the U.S. my mind hummed with the possibilities of starting fresh. I daydreamed about finding a job and sending money home. I could see my mother receiving the cash from Western Union and telling everyone how wrong they were in their opinions of me. Maybe, I'd look into becoming a nurse. Wouldn't everyone be impressed if that happened? I wasn't sure about starting a family with Allen, but perhaps. Happily, no matter how I looked at my situation, it was the start of a big adventure with lots of great outcomes.

The customs clerks in Miami were cordial enough and I was whisked through the line with little bother. During the layover in Miami and then at DFW, I marveled at the size of the complexes, the huge crowds, and the number of white people. For the first time in my life, as a black person, I was in the minority. The airports were like gigantic organisms with constant movement inside as people flowed through the concourses like corpuscles through a body. Anxious that I'd get lost or somehow screw up the voyage, I kept my itinerary close at hand and constantly read the flight status boards to make sure that I was where I was supposed to be.

At another brief layover in Portland, Oregon, I chatted with a fellow traveler, Shannon, a decidedly plump and cheery white woman. Coincidentally, she was also on the way to Olympia. I was excited to make a friend right away, and I gave her the number to Allen's home so we could stay in touch.

At 9:00 PM, fifteen hours after I'd left Jamaica, I arrived at Seatac, Washington. This time of year in the Northwest the weather was quite cold. To show how naive I was about the world, I wore a sleeveless linen pantsuit and hadn't thought of bringing warm clothes. In Jamaica, it was seldom cool enough to be uncomfortable, so the idea hadn't occurred to me to prepare for something I had no experience with—a winter climate.

Allen was waiting in the terminal, and we beamed happily when we saw each other. After such a long trip, I was glad my journey was almost over. When we stepped out of the terminal, icy air blasted over me. By the time we reached his car, I was shivering.

"If you're cold," he opened the car door for me, "why don't you put on a sweater?"

"I don't have any," I replied. "Maybe you brought something?"

He shook his head, then took his place in the driver's seat to start the car. He turned a switch on the dashboard, and welcome heat poured from the vents.

I remarked, "It's a good thing your car has a heater."

Allen smirked. "All cars have heaters. Even the ones in Jamaica."

They did? I didn't even realize that cars had heaters since we never used them on the island.

We drove out of the airport and onto the highway. He pointed out landmarks along the way, but it was all a strange, dizzying blur for me. I couldn't get a grip on where we were; what lay past the streetlamps was shrouded in darkness.

"Are you okay?" Allen asked. "You're pretty quiet."

"This is so different." I gestured out the windshield to a landscape of glaring lights and shadows that shifted around us like a kaleidoscope. "I'm still trying to take it all in."

He squeezed my knee. "Give it time. You'll grow to love it here and won't for a second regret your decision to be with me."

He lived in Olympia, in a modest house by American standards but still much nicer and bigger than what I was used to in Jamaica. We settled in for our first night together in my new home.

The next morning, I padded into the kitchen, eager to demonstrate my cooking skills by making Allen breakfast. "I want to make sure you're well fed before you go to work."

He replied, "I'm not going to work today."

That admission surprised me, and then I realized he hadn't mentioned anything about employment. He seemed to have anticipated my question when he said, "I'm in between jobs right now. It's nothing to worry about."

He left to run errands. While he was gone I tried to call Jamaica to inform my mother that I had arrived safely. But the call wouldn't go through so I figured I must not understand how to make an international call. I spent the rest of the day going through the house and then watching television.

When Allen returned, I said, "I need to call my mother."

Allen frowned. "What for?"

"I want to tell her that I arrived safe."

"You'll get to it."

"Why can't I call her now?" I asked, getting angry.

"I'll tell you why," Allen replied, voice rising. His face reddened. "Because I don't appreciate the way she treated me back in Jamaica. I don't like being humiliated in front of my wife or strangers."

I saw his point about that, but then again, he hadn't told me that his main reason for visiting Jamaica was to do drugs. He was lucky he wasn't tossed in jail, so in receiving a scolding from my mother he got off easy. I kept my tone calm so that I sounded reasonable. "Mother will be worried if I don't call."

"That's her problem."

"You're doing more than hurting her, you're hurting me as well."

Allen stayed quiet.

"I'm your wife. Why did you marry me only to treat me this way?"

"Look, you're not in Jamaica anymore." Allen's expression softened. "This is your new home. Things are different here. If you want to change and learn how to live like an American, then you have to do as I say. I know about these things and you don't."

True, there was much I had to learn about living in America and about being a wife. I reflected on how Mother handled living with my father, and he was probably the most difficult person I knew. Marriage was important to her, and she made it work. So I decided that I was still too new to marriage to put up a fuss, even though I knew Allen was wrong and that he was being petty.

That afternoon, Allen's brother, Dennis, showed up. Though I saw the resemblance between them, Dennis was a little taller and clean-shaven. I also got the sense from him that he acted relieved that Allen had gotten married, even to a Jamaican woman who was so different in appearance and background. Dennis and I were alone in the living room enjoying soft drinks when he said, "So you know, this is my house."

"What do you mean?" I asked.

"I'm letting Allen stay here rent free," Dennis explained. "You see, he owned another house but lost it to pay back debts."

"Debts from what?"

"He borrowed money for drugs."

I couldn't believe this. How much cocaine had Allen consumed that it cost him his house? And after he had lost his house, he still hadn't learned his lesson and kept using drugs. I'd seen other people wreck their lives this way and had kept them at arm's length. Now Allen and his drug habit were a big problem that had fallen into my lap.

"I'm hoping you can keep him steady," Dennis said.

"Steady, how?" I was beginning to see that my relationship with Allen involved more than the usual wifely duties.

"Allen has problems," Dennis answered.

"Besides the drugs?"

"He is a Vietnam war vet. He saw a lot of stuff over there. Stuff he won't talk about. It messed him up pretty bad."

I let that news fit in with what else I'd learned about my husband. "He told me he's in between jobs."

"Allen has trouble holding on to work. Behavioral issues. Doing drugs doesn't help."

I thought about Allen visiting Jamaica. He seemed to have plenty of funds for what he wanted to do. "What does he do for money?"

"The family helps him out as much as we can. It's a shame what happened to him in Vietnam. I mean, he did what the government asked of him and didn't expect to come back the way he did." Dennis fussed with his hands. "By giving him money we hope that keeps him from dealing in drugs. I don't want him roaming the streets."

I nodded, suddenly sympathetic to Allen's plight. His use of cocaine wasn't simply an indulgence, but an escape from a night-mare that wouldn't let go. Begrudgingly, I had to admire him for being so stoic about his problems. "I wouldn't want to see him get hurt."

"It's not him," Dennis explained, "it's other people. Allen can get violent." Dennis lowered his voice. "To be honest, Allen scares us. We're worried that one day he'll snap and go nuts with a gun."

The hair on the back of my neck tingled with alarm. "He has a gun in the house?"

Dennis shook his head. "Not anymore. He used to have several until we made a deal that he turn them over to us in exchange for financial help."

I thought about how easy it had been for Barbara to get that revolver back in Jamaica in spite of the island's strict gun-control laws. "If Allen can get crack, he can surely get a gun."

Dennis sighed, like talking about Allen was an enormous weight that pressed him down. And now a lot of that weight was on my shoulders as well. Dennis gave me his business card. "Keep this handy in case you need my help."

I glanced at the phone number and instantly memorized it. This ability to recall numbers and dates was a skill that was gradu-ally sharpening itself.

After Dennis left, I said to Allen, "I need to call my mother."

Allen scowled. "Not this again. I've already told you no."

"But this has nothing to do with you."

"You're in my house, it has everything to do with me. Now drop it."

I remembered what Dennis had said about Allen's temper, and I worried about provoking my husband to the point that he might hit me, or just as bad, have my visa revoked.

Allen stormed out the door to smoke a cigarette while I retreated to the bedroom. My thoughts turned round and round. Why did everything in my life have to be so complicated? It seemed that every development brought problems that outweighed the promise of better times. I began thinking about Alrick and how he had been taken from me. Now here I was in America, the land of opportunity, and I felt just as constrained as I did in Jamaica.

The phone on the nightstand rang, startling me. Allen must've heard the phone in the front room because he rushed inside and answered it. I listened but the conversation with the caller was muffled and brief.

Allen shouted, "Petergay, it's for you."

Hesitantly, I picked up the handset and answered.

"Petergay," a woman's voice chirped, "It's Shannon, from the airport."

In my mind, her cherubic face appeared, bubbly and friendly. "I hope I didn't catch you at a bad time."

"Not at all." Actually, her call broke the tension that filled the house.

"I'm calling to see if you'd like to go to the movies with me."

I'd never been to a cinema before, and I could use a break from Allen. He watched from the threshold to the bedroom. I cupped the handset to my shoulder and explained that it was Shannon and what she wanted.

Allen shrugged. "Sure. Go ahead." I could tell he also needed a time-out. He opened his wallet and handed me a ten and a twenty.

\*\*\*

Shannon picked me up to see *A Bug's Life*. The movie was a good choice since its laughs helped brighten my mood, and going to the theater was my first chance to experience life in America.

I had a great time and during the ride home I wanted to let Shannon know how special this night had been. It was important that she like me so I offered what would've been a very welcome compliment in Jamaica. I said, "You look fat."

Shannon was certainly well fed, and so what I noted wasn't off the mark.

But the way her face crumpled in hurt told me that I had said the wrong thing. Back in Jamaica, to say someone was fat meant they were healthy enough to put on weight and had the means to do so. Shannon immediately turned as cold as the air outside. I felt so stupid. I'd been in my new home for less than twenty-four hours and had already turned a friend into an enemy.

She dropped me off at my home and that was the last I saw of her.

***

The next day Allen and I left the house for a sightseeing drive. The Northwest proved as green as Jamaica but a different sort of green. The trees were tall pines growing upon rugged hills. In the distance, snow-capped mountains stretched across the horizon. We drove along Puget Sound where the water was a deep, cold blue.

He stopped for gas at a 7-Eleven close to home. Inside I noticed calling cards for sale and I speculated that if I bought one, I could at last call Jamaica. By now I was familiar enough with the surroundings that I could make my way here from Allen's house.

Easier said than done. When at home, Allen kept a close watch on me. I didn't dare slip out when he left because there would be nothing but a mean-spirited argument if I wasn't home when he returned. He didn't have a job and his frequent jaunts out of the house made me guess he earned extra money dealing in drugs.

To get out of the house with his permission I came up with a plan. "I need to exercise," I told him. "I want to keep my figure." At the time, I had a trim yet voluptuous build.

"What kind of exercise?"

I'd seen women jogging around the neighborhood, a strange sight to me since in Jamaica people only ran if they were playing sports or fleeing the law.

"I want to go jogging. If I stay home and do nothing, I'll get fat." From my experience with Shannon, I knew Americans didn't admire fat people.

"That's a good idea," Allen agreed, surprising me since he had been so dismissive of most everything else that I wanted. "I'll buy you running shoes and sweats."

During my initial attempts at running I felt awkward, as I hadn't run in a long time and I'd get winded if I proceeded at a pace faster than a slow jog. Eventually I found a comfortable stride and made my way around the neighborhood. With a twenty-dollar bill tucked in my waistband, I headed to the 7-Eleven and used the entire amount to buy a calling card. But that proved to be only a temporary victory, since getting that card didn't solve my problem about calling Jamaica. I didn't know how to use the card and the line at home remained blocked.

In my jogs through the neighborhood I realized that I was the only black person in the community. The people I met were warm enough but I could tell they regarded me with curiosity at best, suspicion at worst. More than ever, I had to call Jamaica and regain touch with my roots.

Even without Allen's moodiness, the house seemed to shrink about me, and what was at first a welcoming environment was now claustrophobic and oppressive. Boredom set in, and with it came a sense of isolation like I was in a prison. I needed to get out, I needed to breathe, I needed my freedom.

Over dinner, I said to Allen, "I want to get a job."

"What for? I'm taking care of you."

"I could help pay the bills."

"They're getting paid."

"I need to send money home."

"This is your home."

"I need to get out of the house."

He pointed to the door. "You're free to leave."

"That's not what I meant. I need your help to find work."

"Forget it."

"Okay then, what about going to school?"

He clanked his fork on the plate. "I said, forget it. I'm taking care of you." He gestured to the four walls and then the ceiling. "Everything you need is right here."

The problem was, that wasn't true.

# CHAPTER 12

I wasn't surprised when Allen told me we had to go to Roseberg, Oregon, because he had to make a traffic court appearance. By now I realized he was always in some kind of legal jam. Despite this, I looked forward to the trip since it broke up the monotony of staying at the house, plus it gave me the opportunity to see more of the countryside. The trip was a six-hour drive not counting stopping for lunch in Portland. Since Allen's court time was early the next morning, he had planned that we'd spend the night in an economy motel.

By now, Allen didn't bother hiding his drug use from me. Once we settled in the motel room he smoked a pipe of crack and then passed out on the bed.

This was my chance to phone Jamaica. Using the calling card and the motel phone, I had no problem putting the call through. The complication was that Mother had no phone, so I had to call one of her neighbors and have her relay when I'd try again. Knowing that Allen's hit would typically knock him out for an hour, I told the neighbor to expect my call in thirty minutes.

This second time, when I called, I didn't realize Allen had woken up. The phone was on the nightstand right next to the bed so it was obvious what I was doing.

Livid, he shot out of bed and yanked the telephone receiver from my hand to slam it onto the cradle. "Didn't I tell you not to call your mother?" He grabbed my arm and shook me hard. "I oughta throw you into the street and let you spend the night there." His eyes were red-hot rivets of fury, and Dennis' warnings came back to me. I became fearful of Allen's temper and that he'd lose control and hurt me.

"Okay," I said, meekly.

He let go and retreated into the bathroom.

Truly, I was concerned that he was out of his mind and capable of anything. So while he was in the bathroom I called the police.

When Allen came out of the bathroom I kept my distance. He had his hackles up like an angry dog, and I was afraid to get close to him. He lay on the bed to watch the television, a small portable unit, while I sat in a chair off to the side.

About fifteen minutes later, two shadows crossed in front of the room's window curtain, followed by a stern knock. "Roseberg Police."

Allen bolted upright, looking very worried. He glanced to his overnight bag which I knew contained more cocaine. "What are they doing here?"

"I called them." I stood to answer the door.

"What?"

"I was worried about you hitting me."

Two cops were outside. One of them was not much taller than me and he was on the pudgy side. They both craned their necks to look past me into the room. Pudgy Cop said, "We heard there was a disturbance. Mind if we come in?"

Without an invitation, he stepped forward anyway and I

backtracked from him. He and his partner entered and scoped out the room.

"What's the problem?" Tall Cop asked.

"I called," I answered. "My husband was roughing me up."

"Husband?" He lifted an eyebrow and both cops glanced back-and-forth between Allen and me. I could tell they didn't believe we were married. To them, a black woman with a white man in a budget motel spelled serious mischief.

"ID?" Pudgy Cop asked.

Allen smirked at him and replied, "Won't they miss you at the donut shop?"

Pudgy Cop acted as if he hadn't heard the comment.

I handed my passport to Tall Cop. He studied my frizzy black hair and compared my face to the photo on my passport.

"I don't know what she told you," Allen explained as he gave the cop his driver's license. "There's no problem here. We got into an argument about what to watch on the TV."

"That's not true," I replied. "I thought he was going to hurt me." Even as I said this I realized that my thick Jamaican accent wasn't helping my case.

Allen said, "She's new to this country and gets frustrated easily. It's a simple misunderstanding between a husband and wife. You know how it is."

Tall Cop asked me, "Did he hit you?"

"He grabbed my arm."

Allen chuckled. "That was to keep her calm. If she doesn't get her way, she gets pretty hysterical."

Pudgy Cop kept looking around as if to see if anything was out of place. Other than the messed-up bedcovers, the room remained fairly neat. He whispered something to Tall Cop, who was jotting information into a small memo pad.

Tall Cop tapped Allen's ID and my passport against the palm of his hand. I could tell he was mulling what to do. "Okay," he said and returned Allen's ID and my passport. "Whatever disagreements you two have, keep them civil and keep them quiet. We don't want to see you again."

They walked out the door, and Allen closed it behind them. I was fuming at the unfairness even as he gloated. When he got back on the bed, I pulled out my calling card and picked up the phone's handset.

Allen swung off the mattress. "What are you doing?"

"What does it look like I'm doing?"

He clawed for the phone and I kept my back to him. Allen clutched my shoulder and flung me backwards, where I landed on the carpet next to the television. He grabbed the phone and jerked the line out of the wall. "There, try and call home now."

I was filled with such rage that I jumped to my feet and grabbed the closest thing available—the television. Allen was turning away when I heaved it right at his head. He caught the movement and faced me just as the television smashed his nose. He stumbled and collapsed to the floor, blood gushing from his nostrils.

"Damn it!" He clutched his nose and tried to stem the blood. "I'm going to get you."

I searched for another weapon. "Go ahead."

When he staggered upright, I launched myself at him. Snarling like alley cats, we grappled and flailed about the room, knocking over furniture, oblivious to everything but our brawl.

Suddenly, a pair of strong hands pulled me off Allen, and my arms were wrenched back. Cold steel cuffs cinched my wrists.

The two cops from earlier had returned. The motel desk clerk stood by the open door. "I thought they were killing each other."

Tall Cop rolled Allen onto his belly and snapped handcuffs on his wrists. As I was dragged backwards I wanted to scream, but Pudgy Cop twisted my arms in a painful come-along that took the fight completely out of me.

Allen was hauled to his feet. Chest bellowing, he wrestled against his restraints.

Tall Cop jerked the handcuffs. "You gonna settle down?"

Allen gasped and whispered, "Yeah."

"Where's your passport?" Pudgy Cop asked me.

I pointed with my chin. "My purse. On the table."

Allen and I were led from the motel room, both of us smeared with his blood. Out in the parking lot, other guests gaped at us from their open doors. Allen and I were forced into the back of the police car and I realized that we looked like a pair of common criminals. I had come to America for a better life, and in less than a week I was in worse trouble than I'd ever been in Jamaica.

We were taken to the county jail, booked, and locked up. I was issued orange prisoner coveralls and a pair of cheap shower clogs. Afterwards, I sat in a women's holding cell, on a cold steel bunk with a thin mattress, a blanket barely worthy of the name, and a tiny pillow. I kept to myself as I was scared about what could happen next. My cellmates were lowlifes similar to who I'd find in these circumstances in Jamaica—drunks, drug users, prostitutes, and petty criminals—the big difference was that most of them were either white or from one of the local Indian tribes.

I couldn't sleep and kept pestering the jailers for my one phone call. Sometime the next morning they at last let me out of the cell and walked me to a phone down the hall. The jailer stayed by my side and leaned against the wall, close enough to eavesdrop.

From memory, I called Dennis' number.

"It's Petergay, your sister-in-law." I explained what had happened. "Please do me a favor," I begged. "Call this number and ask them to post my bail."

"Who are they?"

"They're Gene and Aznina Czaplinski, a couple that I babysat for back in Jamaica. They'll remember me." I recited the number from memory.

"Got it," Dennis said. "I'll keep you posted."

I hung up the phone and was escorted back to my cell. While I waited for word about bail, my situation didn't improve. My Jamaican passport triggered the attention of the immigration services, and a couple of their officers, Agents Smith and Carlyle, visited the jail to question me in an interrogation room.

"Your passport is fake," Smith accused, "and you're an imposter of another Petergay Dunkley. As soon as we can, we're going to deport you to Jamaica."

"Petergay is a man's name," Carlyle added, his tone heavy with derision as if I, as a foreigner, had stupidly taken a name of the wrong gender. "Come clean about your true identity, and we'll arrange for better accommodations while this situation is resolved."

But the joke was on them, and I wasn't going to let them buffalo me into an admission that wasn't true.

"It is my name," I countered. "You don't believe me, check with the Jamaican embassy. That passport is as authentic as your credentials." I pointed to the ID badge clipped to Carlyle's sport coat.

"Don't waste our time," he replied. "Petergay is a man's name."

"Have you been to Jamaica?"

"Never."

"Then you wouldn't know."

Smith handed me a slip of paper, and on it was written Peter-Gay Dunkley. "Who is this man to you?"

When I read the name, I laughed. "That's not me. That's entirely the wrong person. I don't spell my name that way. Check my passport."

Though Carlyle and Smith tried to act as if they weren't surprised, when they looked at my passport I could tell that indeed, they had overlooked that my name was spelled differently.

"That doesn't change anything." Smith collected the slip of paper and my passport. "We're going to confirm that this is a forged passport and when we do, you'll be deported right away."

When I was returned to my cell, my mood remained glum. The jail cell was as expected: uncomfortable, there was no privacy, and my cellmates were people I wanted no part of. Even if my bail was posted, I wasn't going anywhere until the immigration services cleared me, and the process was dragging into a second day, then a third.

This particular afternoon was memorable because a new prisoner, Sally, was brought in. She was a rough type, skinny and grisly with a weather-beaten complexion, and judging from her attitude, no stranger to spending time in jail. After Sally was locked in with us, she kept tabs on the comings-and-goings of the jailers and I wondered what she was up to. When she determined that the coast was clear, she slipped out of her coveralls and began digging into her crotch. She produced a small plastic bag that contained a packet of cigarettes and a disposable lighter.

Several of the others in the cell snickered in delight. Sally passed out cigarettes—I refused—and within a minute, they defiantly puffed away despite the "No Smoking" placards on the walls. I knew their smoking party wouldn't last long, but I guess the point was that every drag on their cigarettes was a finger to the system.

When the jailers returned, they couldn't help but notice the tobacco smoke.

"Put those out!" one of them shouted.

The women kept smoking until the jailers burst into the cell and plucked the cigarettes from their lips and collected them in a mop bucket. The jailers made us stand along the bars while they searched our steel bunks and patted us each down.

"Where did you get these cigarettes?"

Sally and the rest shrugged.

A jailer turned to me. "Petergay, come along."

He and another jailer led me to the interrogation room where he demanded, "How did you sneak those cigarettes in here?"

"Why are you asking me? You didn't catch me smoking and I don't smoke."

"Then who did?"

I was positive that in America, as in Jamaica, no one liked a snitch. While I didn't owe Sally anything, likewise I didn't owe the jailers anything either. "I don't know."

"Listen, we can make your life here miserable."

"More miserable than it is?"

The jailer resented me standing my ground like I did. Once

back in the cell, Sally regarded me with suspicion. I returned her glare with a sharp glower of my own to let her know that I didn't appreciate getting into trouble on her account.

The next morning, Sally and her friends lit up again. As before, the jailers stormed in and confiscated the cigarettes. This time their search was more thorough as they weren't going to be embarrassed by overlooking the stash of cigarettes a second time. For their efforts, all they found was the empty pack and the disposable lighter by the toilet, a common area, so they couldn't accuse anyone of possessing this contraband. The pack and the lighter were dumped into the mop bucket and then tossed in the trash.

And again, I was taken to the interrogation room.

The jailer shoved me inside. "Tell us what you know. Who smuggled the cigarettes?"

"Since when it is my job to watch the others? That's your job." By now I was certain I'd been singled out because of my very dark skin, and I was Jamaican.

I had no idea how long my stay in this horrible jail was going to last. I began to hate Sally and the others, since they acted like smuggling in the cigarettes and lighting up was a great accomplishment, but it was nothing to be proud of.

I was stewing in a bored funk when a jailer approached the cell. "Petergay. Phone call."

Instantly, my hopes lifted. Was the call about my bail? Then another thought tempered my mood. Maybe it was the immigration services calling with bad news.

The jailer unlocked the door and escorted me down the hall to the booking room. He pointed to a phone on the counter. I picked up the handset and answered tentatively. "This is Petergay."

"This is Dennis." I recognized his voice. "Your friends are going to post bail. You should be out this afternoon."

*Hallelujah.*

Another problem. After I left the jail, where was I going to stay? I couldn't stay with Allen, once he was released. I explained my dilemma to Dennis.

"I thought of that," he replied. "You can stay with my mother."

"No, I can't impose," I protested, though I was relieved by that news.

"She's expecting you."

"So what's next?" I asked.

"When I hear bail has been posted, I'll come get you."

I returned to the cell, giddy with anticipation that I'd soon be leaving this hellhole. Within a couple of hours I was taken back to the booking area, where my clothes were returned. Attached to my release form was a letter where Agent Smith had signed off that my passport was legitimate, and it was also returned to me. A condition of my release was that I had to remain available and ready to appear in court. If I failed, my friends would be out their bail money and the court would issue a warrant for my arrest, which definitely meant certain deportation after jail time.

At the moment, Allen remained incarcerated as no one would post his bail. Dennis drove me to Allen's house so I could retrieve my belongings. As I collected them I got wistful that my marriage to Allen had fallen apart so quickly. However, I was in the U.S. and remained determined to find success here.

Dennis drove me to his mother's house where I met Gail, and she treated me like a cherished daughter-in-law, instead of as an accomplice to Allen and his troublemaking. She kindly showed me an extra room that I could call my own until I was ready to move on.

"It's a shame that Allen can't be with anyone without pulling them down," Gail later said over coffee. "That's why we've learned to keep our distance. And it's a shame to treat one's son that way."

I agreed but Allen was a grown man and responsible for his own life. Now that I had a safe place to stay, my next priority was to earn my keep. "Gail, could you help me find a job?"

"You'll first need a Social Security card," she answered. "I'll take you to their office tomorrow."

Since I had a temporary resident's visa, that was enough to qualify me for a Social Security card. With that in hand, I noticed that the McDonald's on the way to Gail's house was hiring. I had her drop me off, and upon applying was quickly hired. I coordinated my work schedule to accommodate her daily commute

I called home as often as I could but kept a positive spin on what I told Mother.

One night after dinner, Gail answered the phone. She exclaimed, "Allen!" and her brows knitted during the short but intense conversation. Turning pale and looking very worried, she hung up the phone. "He says he's going to get back at us for colluding against him."

"That's ridiculous," I replied. "No one is against him."

"You don't know Allen," she said. "He has crazy ideas about the way the world works. He wants to make you pay and if any of the rest of us interfere, we'll get hurt too."

My situation felt like a trap closing around me.

Then I couldn't stay. I had better leave as soon as possible.

# CHAPTER 13

With Allen's threats echoing in my head, I knew the clock was ticking before he brought disaster down upon his family and me. I had to get away from him. In the phone book I found a brochure for the Battered Person's Advocacy and contacted them about my situation. Without hesitation, they offered shelter and counseling. I packed up what little I had and Dennis' wife drove me to the shelter, a nondescript building south of downtown.

Jackie, the head of the shelter, greeted me, and we sat in her office while she documented my case. She was an older woman, bright, pleasant, and very understanding of my plight.

At the moment, I had two big concerns. The first was Allen's threats against me, and the second was my upcoming court date. Regarding Allen, Jackie filed a restraining order on my behalf against him. And she and her staff helped me prepare for my court appearance.

I was grateful that I had such a network of competent and caring people on my side. I could tell by the furnishings in Jackie's office—mismatched furniture, handcrafted decorations, worn carpet—that the Advocacy operated on a shoestring budget, but their lack of money did not dampen their enthusiasm or commitment.

Unfortunately, I was only one of several other women seeking help at the shelter. The youngest looked like a teenager still in middle school though she cradled a baby. Another woman appeared in her sixties, with a face etched with deep wrinkles from a life of hard knocks.

I was given clothes and toiletries and issued a cot and bedding. Jackie emphasized that this shelter was temporary and that I had to move on as soon as I could, which I was eager to do.

One bright spot was that I could use my calling cards with the shelter's phone and call my mother in Jamaica. During my first call to her I mentioned that Allen and I had separated.

"I'm not surprised," she replied. "Now what are your plans?"

"To keep working."

"In Washington?"

Her question made me consider that I should move somewhere that I felt more at home. "Where else could I go?"

"We have relatives in Florida," Mother said. "You might have better opportunities there, and you'll be among your people."

That and I'd be far away from Allen. I was overcome with gratitude that my mother was always looking out for me. Her offer carried a tone of optimism, like things were going to turn out all right. "Yes, Mother, see what you can do."

Despite her hopeful words, the night before my court appearance I tossed and turned in my bed, unable to sleep from worry. So much could go wrong. The judge might decide to throw me in jail for hitting Allen with the television. He might also decide that I had violated the conditions of my visa and have me deported.

All I wanted was the chance to prove that I was a good person and able to work and contribute to society. Yet since my adolescence, at every step toward that goal I had somehow tripped and fallen into trouble.

The next morning, I dressed in my best clothes. Jackie drove me to the court and together we signed in.

"What about Allen?" I asked, anxiously. "He's going to be here as well."

"Don't worry," Jackie said. "The court has deputies and guards to protect you. Besides, if Allen tries anything while in court, that will only work to your advantage to demonstrate that he's a threat to you."

A nice bit of advice, but of little worth if Allen were to stab me with whatever weapon he might be able to smuggle in. I'd heard plenty of stories of what people did on their way to jail.

Allen wasn't my only cause for distress. An officer from Immigration Services was waiting for me. He said, "Depending on the outcome, I might have to deport you."

His warning confirmed my deepest fears and so scared me that I began shaking. I told Jackie, "I just want to go to the shelter, get my things, and run away."

Jackie took my hand. "Things will work out. Trust me."

A bailiff opened the courtroom door and ordered us inside. At the far end of the courtroom, a judge waited at his bench. As we walked toward him, I was overwhelmed by the moment. I could sense the immense weight of the government's machinery bearing upon me. I recalled that term, *the wheels of justice*, and imagined them as gigantic gears ready to grind me into pulp and then churn back what little was left.

Jackie and I halted at a table in front of the judge.

Allen arrived, by himself. He wore nice clothes and had cleaned himself up so he looked respectable. But my mouth went dry at the sight of him, and I became tense with apprehension. He nodded to acknowledge me and took his place at the next table over.

The two cops who arrested Allen and me also showed up, and at the sight of them I was sure I was done for.

Jackie sensed my trepidation. "Petergay," she whispered, "relax. Don't fret about what can happen until it does."

We remained standing while the judge completed signing a stack of papers. Our case was one of several that he had scheduled for the day.

He looked about 50, with a crown of dark hair around his shiny bald pate. He set his pen aside and ordered us to take a seat. He requested that Allen and I identify ourselves, and Jackie chimed in to inform the judge who she was.

He read the charges against us both and asked Allen to make a statement. Basically, he repeated what he had told the cops the night we'd been arrested, that I was the one who had provoked the argument and then attacked him. I remembered how the police had accepted his word, and I became uneasy with dread that the judge was going to come down hard on me.

The judge asked if the cops had anything to add besides what was in their report. They said no.

The judge turned to me. "Ms. Dunkley, have you anything to say?"

Jackie prodded me in the side that I stand. All my life, male authority figures had been quick to dismiss me, and I saw no reason why this would be different. No matter what I said, I was convinced that the verdict was in and my comments were little more than theater.

"Your Honor," I began, voice trembling, "I am sorry for any trouble that I have caused. Though I am new to this country, I know the difference between right and wrong. Fighting with my husband was wrong, but I do have a right to defend myself, which is what I did that night. All I want is a chance to take advantage of the opportunities that this great country offers and to become a productive and useful citizen." I had explained myself as honestly as I could, but I was certain that my thick Jamaican accent was working against me.

The judge scribbled into his notebook.

"But there is more," I said.

"Oh?" The judge lifted his eyes.

I continued. "What the report doesn't say is that Allen was high that night and that he made fun of one of the cops—" I pointed at Pudgy Cop— "because of his weight."

"Is that true?" the judge asked.

In an embarrassed voice, Pudgy Cop answered, "Yes, Your Honor."

The judge addressed Allen. "Didn't you plead guilty for harassing Ms. Dunkley, your wife?"

Allen stood and replied, "Yes, Your Honor."

The judge considered this, then leaned over his bench toward me. "Ms. Dunkley, I find you not guilty. The charges against you are dismissed. Welcome to the United States of America, and good luck in whatever career you choose." With a great flourish, he signed the papers releasing me. "You are free to go."

I was so lightheaded with disbelief that I could hardly stand. Jackie hugged me to keep me from falling over.

Returning to the shelter, I called Mother and shared the great news.

"I have news, too," she said. "Your cousin Penny in Miami has an apartment where you can stay." Mother gave me the phone number.

Penny readily made me feel welcome with his cheery voice and optimistic tone. This was one good aspect of Jamaican culture; the door was always open for visitors.

"However, I won't be in Miami when you show up," Penny said. "But no problem, here's the address of the restaurant that my land-lord owns. I'll leave my apartment key with the manager."

I'd saved enough money from my job at McDonald's for a Greyhound bus ticket from Portland to Miami. When I told Mother of my travel plans, she noted, "You should be in Miami tomorrow."

"Mother, the trip will take four days."

"What are you talking about?"

In Jamaica, you can cross the island by bus in half a day, and so she had no idea just how big of a country the United States was. "Trust me, Mother, when you visit me, you'll see."

The day of my departure, I gathered the belongings the shelter had given me, which included a hairdryer. Jackie drove me to the bus station, and bade me goodbye and offered the best of luck.

The bus ride was an ordeal. We were packed in tight and forced to make do with our cramped seating for hours at a time. On and on we drove. From the cold wet forests of the Northwest, over the snowy Rocky Mountains and through great deserts that amazed me with their vast emptiness. We crossed through the wooded hills of Texas and the South. America was huge and the highway seemed without end. It never occurred to me until now that you could spend that much time on a bus and still not get where you're going.

When I saw my first Florida license plate I thought that our next stop was going to be Miami. Eight hours and several stops later, we finally reached the city.

After I left the bus, I took a taxi for the Jamaican restaurant to pick up the key to Penny's apartment. When I arrived, I introduced myself to the manager and he promptly gave me the key to my cousin's one-bedroom apartment in South Miami.

When I entered the apartment, I was overcome with a sense of relief. So much had happened in the brief time since I'd come to America, and I'd even managed to cross the big country coast-to-coast. Once settled in the apartment I wandered about the neighborhood. I found a market that sold chicken parts for cheap, which I bought along with a bag of rice. After I returned to the apartment, I left the door open to let air circulate as was the custom back on Jamaica. A woman whom I recognized as one of the next-door neighbors peered at me through the doorway.

"For your safety you need to keep this door closed," she cautioned. "This is Miami, not Jamaica."

Two weeks later my cousin Penny arrived, and it filled me with so much joy to finally meet with family, even if we hardly knew each other. Penny was a wiry bundle of energy with an eager smile. However, when I told him my story, he cried like a baby.

"You went through such an awful time," he said. "And I'm glad to help you. But you need to know that I'm returning to Jamaica at the end of the month so you have to find a place of your own before then."

In that case I needed rent money, which meant finding a job. In a neighborhood newspaper I found an ad that said, *Be your own boss. Prestige Marketing.* I called, and they sounded eager to hire me.

The company resided in an office in a strip mall a bus ride from the apartment. I met the owner/manager and he seemed sincerely glad that I was interested in his company. In his mid-thirties, tall and wearing a cheap tie and high-water pants, he spoke with a certainty and determination that reminded me of an evangelical church pastor. During the short interview, he emphasized the tremendous opportunities if I was willing to apply myself.

Basically, I was to go door-to-door selling inexpensive merchandise like knives, kitchen utensils, and toys. The owner related in grandiose ways how it was possible to earn hundreds of dollars a day. When I heard that I wondered, if it was that easy to make so much money, why did his office look so run down and why didn't he wear nicer clothes?

I kept these questions to myself and was hired right away. I returned early the next day where I met about a dozen other employees for our morning meeting. The owner assigned us our territories for the day, and then launched into a dramatic motivational sermon like he was a street preacher trying to prepare us for battle against Satan. At the end of it we'd shout together:

"Dream big, earn big."

"Today is when magic happens."

"Quitters never win. Winners never quit."

All of us would leave those meetings pumped up and ready to conquer the world. But the enthusiasm didn't last, especially after I'd done this drill several times. For every ten dollars that I made, I only kept $1.50. Usually, after a long day of pounding the pavement and getting doors slammed in my face, I would pocket fifteen dollars, and the most I ever kept was $42. The constant and demoralizing rejection aside, I was working too hard for too little money.

I gleefully quit my job with Prestige Marketing and applied at the Denny's in Miami's South Beach, at the corner of Collins and 29th Street. The job they offered was as a hostess, which surprised me since I was from Jamaica, somewhat shy, and still uncertain about my looks. I continued to harbor lingering feelings that I wasn't attractive. The Denny's manager gave me one day of training and set me loose, assigning me the worst shift of all, the busy and boisterous night shift.

No surprise, I promptly got in hot water. I'd been instructed to never sit anyone in the reserved area. So what happened? A group of police officers came in and took their places right there. When I told them to move, they responded with astonished looks like I didn't know what I was talking about. Then one very tall and handsome man led a party of his friends as if they were royalty to the same reserved area. As with the cops, I didn't hesitate to ask them to move.

"Do you know who I am?" he asked.

"It doesn't matter who you are," I replied. "You can't sit here."

His friends snickered at me like I was some daft country girl, which deep down I was, actually.

The shift manager heard the commotion and intervened. "Petergay, don't you know who this is? He's Alonzo Morning, the basketball star."

At the time his name didn't mean anything, but I gathered that he was a local big shot.

"The reserved seating is for him and the police," the shift manager continued.

None of this had been explained to me earlier, but even so, I was made to feel like this misunderstanding had been my fault.

However, the worst part about this job was the night shift itself, because I had to deal with drunks and assorted louts who gave me the creeps from the time I clocked in until the time I clocked out.

During the bus ride to work I made friends with a fellow commuter, an older black woman. One evening I complained to her, "I hate my job at Denny's."

"You want a new job?"

"You know of one?"

"Sure. The KFC close to my house is hiring."

That's all I needed to hear. That night I quit my job at Denny's and the next day applied at the KFC my friend had told me about. Unfortunately, the ride there took three bus transfers. What I didn't realize was that, unlike in Jamaica where you need a referral for any job, here in the U.S. you can simply walk into any place and apply. During every commute I passed several KFCs, and it never occurred to me that I could've applied with them and saved myself the ridiculously long commute. If it rained, I didn't bother with an umbrella since in the hot weather I'd dry out by the time I got to my destination.

I was paid $540 a month, and though it wasn't much, it was enough to save up a deposit so I could take over the lease of my cousin's apartment. The neighborhood was dark and scary when I got home after work, and it didn't help that the streets and sidewalks were overrun with sketchy homeless people.

To stretch my pay, I'd take chicken the KFC was about to toss out and cook it at home with curry to make it taste different. For my commute, I'd fill a large cup with soda. My plan was to save money for a car and send some via Western Union to my family in Jamaica.

My daily routine was tough. The commute to and from the KFC took a lot of time. Since this was a big city, I had to be on guard the entire trip against people with bad intentions and remain mindful that I didn't miss my bus connections. At work I started as a cashier; I diligently applied myself but apparently not hard enough because I'd hear, "C'mon Petergay, you're working way too slow. We're on Miami time, not island time."

Because of that I was reassigned to making sandwiches. Here as well, I was told that I wasn't working fast enough, though in my mind I was slapping those sandwiches together in no time at all.

The weeks stretched into months. I turned 20. Little by little I was building up my savings. Slowly, I seemed to be making headway. During this time and with the help of the Advocacy I divorced Allen, and with that, I thought he could no longer meddle in my life.

But I was wrong.

# CHAPTER 14

Since my residency card was about to expire, the INS had been sending my renewal card to Allen's home in Olympia. Out of spite and petty vengeance, he cut the card into four pieces and mailed them to my mother with a note stating that he hoped I'd get deported.

I called the Battered Person's Advocacy in Roseberg and asked them to again help me. They wrote a letter to the INS explaining my situation, and on the two-year mark of when my residency card was about to expire, I was given an appearance date at their Miami office to apply for a new card. But on the day of my appointment I couldn't find my old card in time and so I arrived too late to apply for a renewal. However, the office issued a stamped letter verifying that I had been there.

I was nervous about what to expect. A few days letter I received a letter explaining that because I had not showed up for the appointment, I had thirty days to leave the country or I'd get deported.

The news shocked me, and I felt pressed into a corner. Because I'd misplaced my green card, my fate had fallen into Allen's hands. Once more, I turned to my friends at the Battered Person's Advocacy.

My call was referred to Jackie. "Petergay, I hope you're going to tell me all went okay with the INS."

"I only wish that was so. I'm afraid I messed up." I proceeded to tell her about the situation that ensued from my missing the appointment.

"That's not good," she said, and I could hear the frustration in her voice. Because of my recent appeals for the Advocacy's help, I felt like their problem child and someone who couldn't take care of herself. Jackie continued, "I can write a letter for you, but at this point you need legal help."

That sounded ominous. "What kind of legal help?"

"You need to hire an immigration lawyer."

A lawyer. *Sigh*. I was sure one would not run cheap. I'd been trying so hard to save money, and now because of my dithering and carelessness, I might have to deplete my hard-earned savings to simply stay put. "Where would I find such a lawyer?"

"I'm sure there are plenty in the Miami area," Jackie answered. "Take my letter and all your INS documents when you make an appointment. Good luck."

Since I'd heard stories about people getting ripped off by shady lawyers, I asked around before deciding on an attorney. Just as Jackie had suggested, you couldn't throw a rock in Miami without hitting an immigration lawyer. Based on the recommendation from a neighbor, I contacted Guzman Gonzales, a Cuban attorney who had a reputable practice in the community.

We met in his office. Though he greeted me warmly enough, when we got down to business he proved to be formal and somewhat stiff, which I appreciated since I wanted a very serious-minded individual handling my case. As I explained my situation he sorted through my papers. After a moment, he set them aside.

"In your case," he said, "we will file an injunction that will stop the INS clock as we submit an appeal."

"What are my chances?" I asked.

He gave a slight shrug. "While I can't speak for the government, your case is not unusual, and I don't see a reason why they shouldn't issue you a new residency card."

"How much is this going to cost me?"

Without blinking, he answered, "Fifteen hundred dollars."

I was dismayed by the amount but had no choice. I lived frugally and diligently saved money, which despite my good intentions, was now practically wiped out. "What does that pay for?"

He waved his hand over my papers. "My filing an injunction and following up with the INS to the point they decide to renew your residency card."

I thought about what he just said. "What if they decide not to renew my card?"

"In that case, we'll file an appeal."

"Which will cost more money?"

Gonzales nodded. "Yes. But let's not get ahead of ourselves. Let us remain positive and not worry about the negative until it happens."

"Okay," I replied. Though not happy that this process might prove even costlier than what it was, I was reassured by his positive attitude.

"Before I can proceed," he said, "I'll need a cashier's check for the fifteen hundred." He pushed his business card and a contract toward me across the desk. "Have the check made out to my firm."

I signed the contract and took his card. The next day I returned with a cashier's check and he promptly filed the injunction. Within two weeks we heard back from the INS, and I received a new residency card with my immigration status changed from conditional to permanent. I studied this card for a long moment and relished the peace of mind that it represented.

With my immigration status worries behind me—and free from Allen's clutches—I moved into a new apartment. But a different address meant I had to sort out my commuting schedule. One morning I was running late and just missed the last bus to get to work on time. I became angry and frustrated with myself. I wasn't making enough money to have such a complicated life.

As I stood on the sidewalk and fretted about how I was going to get to work, a short man with a pencil mustache approached. Interestingly, though he was definitely Cuban he looked much different than the lawyer Gonzales. Whereas the lawyer wore a nice suit and projected a composed and controlled demeanor, this man—*Guayabera* stretched tight over his belly, a stained straw hat perched over thin hair, worn shoes—was definitely someone comfortable with the loose ends of his life.

"You need a ride?" He pointed to his Toyota compact.

"Are you a taxi?"

He grinned. "Not officially. But I am cheaper."

A voice in my head warned me but I had to get to work. I gave him the location of my KFC and asked, "How much?"

"Four dollars." He returned to his car and opened the front passenger door.

Though more expensive than bus fare, the price was affordable. Plus, we would be driving through the middle of town so I could jump out if he caused trouble. When I got in, we exchanged names. His was Juan Fuentes.

Sitting this close, I smelled the cigar smoke clinging to him. Though the car was an older model, the interior was neat and clean. A tiny Cuban flag hung from his rearview mirror. The dashboard bore tiny cracks, and homemade covers draped over the front seats.

"Why don't you just drive a regular cab?" I asked.

"Because this way, the money I make, I keep." He turned the air conditioning to maximum. "Besides, I love this little car."

Fuentes drove straight to the KFC and I got there faster than had I taken the bus. After easing against the curb, he handed me a slip of paper with his phone number. "Call me whenever you need a ride."

His cheap rates and efficient trips through town meant that I frequently came to rely on him. One morning I jumped into his car without realizing that I didn't have any cash.

"Don't worry," he assured me. "You're a good customer. Pay me the next time."

During our short trips, we chatted quite a bit. Though I wasn't in the least attracted to him, I enjoyed our conversations. He was easy to talk to and since he was a fellow transplant to the U.S., I could relate to his stories and insights. Besides driving this unregistered cab, he also worked in a Cuban restaurant.

We rolled through traffic choking on exhaust fumes that made the hot, humid air seem that much more oppressive. We cruised past gleaming high rises and streams of people rushing toward work or some other urgent appointment. In contrast to the bustle, mobs of the marginalized and unemployed loitered in unkempt clusters.

Fuentes pointed toward a knot of homeless. "The American Dream, no?"

I didn't know if he said that to slight them or ridicule the idea of this country as the land of opportunity. Since I'd been homeless, I kept my opinion to myself.

"But whatever, it's better than back home, no?" Fuentes elaborated. "In Cuba, I used to see doctors drive taxis like I do now just to buy a little more than what crumbs the government gives you."

"Life is hard," I agreed. But I was determined to get ahead. I'd gone too far in my life to turn back.

He later picked me up after work from KFC and as usual, I had my takeout dinner on my lap. We were on the highway chatting pleasantly when he suddenly reached over and squeezed my thigh. His touch so alarmed me that I grabbed a plastic fork from the dinner pack and jabbed it deep into his leg.

Yelping in pain, he recoiled from me and shrieked, "Why did you stab me?"

To ward off another advance, I menaced him with the fork. "Why did you grab me?" I realized that he had chosen the highway to make his move since I couldn't jump out without seriously hurting myself. On the other hand, if I made too much of a disturbance, he risked wrecking his car, which was his pride and joy.

Blood seeped through the holes in his pants where I had stabbed him. He slowed and massaged his injured leg. "I'm going to report this and get you deported."

I didn't need any more hassles with immigration and I didn't need any trouble with Fuentes. "Let me out," I demanded. He turned off at the next exit and as soon as I could, I slipped out and ran to the sidewalk bus stop.

But Fuentes wasn't done with me. "I know where you live," he shouted, his face livid like it was going to pop. "I'm going to make your life hell."

A bus approached and Fuentes had to drive off to make way. "You'll pay!" he shouted once more before disappearing into traffic. Though I didn't know where this particular bus was going, I boarded it anyway to hide from Fuentes should he return.

To avoid him, the next day I asked one of my coworkers, Delores, if I could stay with her. "My apartment is getting worked on," I explained since I didn't want to relate my problems with Fuentes. I also didn't want Delores to worry that he would track me to her place.

Once I felt that things had cooled off, I returned to my apartment. My luck changed for the better: when I filed my income taxes, I learned I was due a refund of $1,800. I used that money as a down payment on a Mitsubishi Galant, and with that car, I no longer needed to ride the bus and so I could stay clear of Fuentes.

Or so I thought.

He began calling me regularly and always said the same thing, "You owe me money."

Which was true. On the other hand, the small debts I owed him had been erased when he grabbed my leg and by his subsequent harassment.

One morning I was driving on Interstate 95 when my cellphone chimed. It was Fuentes.

I picked up and launched right into why he was calling. "It's about the money, right?" Before he could say anything, I added, "The restaurant where you work, I'll leave the money with them. Okay?"

Instead of agreeing to that, he replied, "Petergay, let's meet and talk about what you did."

His tone sounded contrite and soft compared to his usual vindictive tone. I decided that he wanted more than just his money. He must've thought that I'd be apologetic about hurting him and would then let him touch me.

The situation threatened to box me in and I had to escape. "Look, Juan, you'll get your money. And then you need to leave me alone."

"Petergay, don't be this way. So you owe me money, we can come to an agreement."

I wanted no part of any agreement with him. As he spoke I veered onto the next exit and turned around to head north toward Fort Lauderdale. My reaction was purely instinctive. I was done hassling with immigration and with Fuentes. While he kept chattering, I ended the call in mid-sentence and wondered why it had taken me so long to do so.

On and on I drove. I got into the habit of packing extra clothes in the trunk of my car, probably a reaction to my sudden episodes of having to run off and leave everything behind. What few possessions that remained in my apartment, I could try to recover later, or abandon if I had to completely start over.

Reaching Fort Lauderdale, I took Exit 29B at Sunrise Boulevard and stopped at the first gas station, where I asked directions to the closest KFC. Afterwards, I drove there straightaway and asked for the manager. A short fellow in a company-issued short-sleeve shirt and tie, he dashed from behind the counter.

"What's the matter?" he asked, nervous like I was about to complain about his establishment.

I smiled to calm him. "I just moved here and would like to apply for a job."

His expression morphed from concern to curiosity. "You have experience?"

"I've been working at the KFC in South Miami." I gave him the address. "Call them for references."

He thought about what I had just told him. "Give me a minute." He walked me to an empty table and handed over an application. "In the meantime, please fill this out."

He entered his office, and I watched him make a phone call. A few minutes later, he returned to my table with pages the other KFC had faxed over. The manager sat beside me and looked pleased that a diligent worker like myself had simply walked in. He reviewed my application and then asked, "Can you start tomorrow?"

"Not a problem."

Just like that, I'd left my problems behind in Miami and found a new job. Feeling the need to reward and pamper myself, I checked into a motel for the night. But considering my tight finances— I had just paid the month's rent for my Miami apartment—this would be the last time in a while that I could indulge in such accommodations.

So, for the next week I lived out of my car and was again homeless. I parked overnight at the Walmart at the corner of Oakland Park and University Boulevard. For breakfast I headed over to the closest McDonald's, where I'd use their bathroom to freshen up for the day.

During this time, I made friends with my fellow coworkers, to include Angela, a woman from the local Jamaican community.

"Where are you staying?" she asked.

I was not at all embarrassed when I told her, "I'm living out of my car."

"You don't have to do that," she replied. "You can sublet a room from me."

"How much?"

"Three hundred and fifty dollars."

I did the arithmetic in my head. If I slept in my car for eight days I could save enough to move in with her.

"But there's no furniture," she explained. "Not even a bed."

"Don't worry about me," I said. "A roof and four walls is better than my car and the parking lot."

I bought an inflatable mattress to sleep on. The package said it was as comfortable as a regular bed, which wasn't true, but staying in Angela's apartment did let me sleep with greater peace of mind. Fortunately, I didn't have to subject myself to the inflatable mattress for long, as I made arrangements to recover my furniture from my old apartment in Miami. With my things and a permanent address, I no longer felt like a vagabond.

Angela invited me to a potluck hosted by some of her friends. This was the first such event I'd attended since coming to America and I was surprised to see so many Jamaicans living in Fort Lauderdale. At the party, I made my rounds and since our shared homeland was but a small island, it wasn't long before I made connections to people I knew.

However, I couldn't afford to get complacent about my life. I wasn't making much money, and that was a condition I had to change right away.

# CHAPTER 15

The need to make more money obsessed me. On my way to Walmart I'd pass a Party City and one morning I noticed a sign in its window: *Now hiring a card person.*

I didn't know what a card person was but that didn't keep me from walking in and speaking to the manager, Carol Dell, about the job. She explained that I'd have to stock and sell cards and blow up balloons. The tasks sounded simple, but the position didn't pay much and I'd only work part time, which meant I had to keep my job at KFC.

Once I started at Party City, I realized that I didn't enjoy the work and putting in all these hours at two jobs. After a couple of weeks, Carol called me into her office. I was worried that my reluctance about this job was showing and that she was going to fire me.

"Petergay," she began.

I held my breath, expecting the worst.

She continued, "I'm really impressed by your work ethic. You always show up on time and pay attention to what you're doing. I really appreciate how you treat the customers."

Her words floored me. I was only doing what she paid me to do and the work was easy, if tedious.

"We'd like to offer you the position of assistant manager. It's full time and you'll get a raise from $6.25 to $8.50 an hour."

I'd only barely recovered from my surprise when I replied, "Yes, I'll take the job."

I was walking on clouds when I returned to the KFC and gave notice. Though I was very proud of myself for the promotion to assistant manager, in truth I didn't find the new position that satisfying but I stuck with it for the experience. One worrisome task was the morning walk when I had to take the previous day's cash and checks to deposit at the bank. This being Fort Lauderdale, if any lowlife knew I was carrying several hundred dollars in loose bills and change, I doubt I would've made it across the parking lot without getting robbed or worse.

With my increase in pay I moved into a large two-bedroom apartment that seemed like a mansion to me. I could make extra money by subleasing the second bedroom, which I rented to Beverly, another woman in the Jamaican community. With this big apartment and a car of my own, I felt rich. I no longer had to eat KFC food, and during the holidays I could work all the overtime I wanted.

Every other week I stopped by American Cash Express to wire money to my mother via Western Union. Because of my regular visits I became friends with one of the cashiers. As I waited for her to process my money order, I asked, "Joanna, how much do you make here?"

"Ten dollars an hour."

Wow, all she did was sit in a booth and handle money. I could do that and not have to hassle with menial work like I was doing at Party City. "Do you think you could get me a job here?"

"I'll ask. Come back tomorrow."

The next day I returned and spoke with Rudy, the franchise owner. I told him about my managerial experience with Party City and he readily offered me a job. Without hesitation I quit Party City, but the amount of money I was making turned out to be a wash. On one hand, I was paid more per hour at my new job, but on the other there was no overtime.

My duties at American Cash Express were easy enough as long as I didn't lose track of the money passing through my hands. When I was processing a particular woman's paycheck I couldn't help but notice that her take-home pay was twice that of mine.

"What is it that you do?" I asked.

"I'm an LPN."

"What's that?"

"A Licensed Practical Nurse."

I immediately thought back to the time in Jamaica when I met a nurse and was stricken with the idea of becoming one myself.

"Is it hard to become a nurse?" I asked.

My customer gathered her cash. "The course is very hard. Don't even think about it."

With that comment, I forgot about becoming a nurse. For now.

While my job at American Cash Express was okay, I wondered if I could make more someplace else. I visited a nearby The Check Cashing Store and chatted up one of the cashiers. Although I still felt shy, one skill that I'd honed on the streets of Jamaica was that if I could talk one-on-one with someone, I could figure them out and establish a good rapport. I asked her how much she made, and she replied, "Eleven dollars an hour."

I couldn't help but keep pushing. "Could you hook me up with a job here?"

"Sure, I'll have you talk to the manager."

I arranged for an interview even though I didn't have a résumé. The manager was another Jamaican woman and I was certain that if I could speak with her, I could talk myself into a job. Just as I hoped, she was impressed enough to offer me a job, starting at $11.25 an hour. The work was pleasant and it helped that I liked both my manager and my fellow employees.

Three years passed by and during that time I made friends with a regular customer, Richard Mahoney. His weekly paycheck was larger than my bi-weekly salary.

"Richard, what do you do?"

"I'm an LPN."

Now this was three times in my life that I'd run into a nurse, and so maybe God was telling me to make my move.

"Is the course hard?" I asked. "Tell me the truth."

"I won't lie, it is hard." Then his eyes locked with mine. "But you can do it."

"All right, I'll think about it."

And think about it I did, but that's all I did.

Every time Richard came in, he'd ask, "So Petergay, have you started the nursing course?"

Though his question was friendly, I could feel the barbed point of the comment prodding me to get off my butt. At last I called the nursing program at a local community college and asked about enrolling.

The woman on the phone explained, "First, you need a high school diploma or a GED."

I didn't have a high school diploma so I asked, "What's a GED?"

"It's the equivalent of a high school diploma."

I hung up without thinking to ask where I'd get a GED. Since it was the equivalent of a diploma, I visited the nearby high school and walked into the office, saying that I wanted to enroll to get my diploma. The receptionist looked me up and down and inquired how old I was.

"Twenty-four."

Her face cracked into a smile. "You're too old for high school."

I knew I sounded naive but I needed information. "Then what do I do? I want to start a nursing course and first I need a high school diploma or a GED."

"Let me show you how this works." She gave me a list of places that offered GED prep courses.

From that I list I selected Atlantic Vocational Tech and paid them a visit. They gave me an assessment test and from those results, recommended some tutoring classes, which I took. After a second assessment test, they decided that I was ready to challenge the GED. I paid $5 for the exam, and after taking it, within a week I received a GED certificate and a letter congratulating me for passing. With the GED in hand, I returned to Atlantic Vocational Tech to apply for the nursing school.

Then I hit a snag. The waiting list for their nursing program was three years long. I simmered in frustration, for I was stalled at the brink of my next big step forward. I checked with another school and found that though their waiting list was only a year long, their tuition was far beyond what I could afford. Through word-of-mouth in the Jamaican community I learned of another nursing school, one located in Pompano Beach—JLF University and run by a Haitian immigrant, Joseph Lafortune—that was not only within my budget but offered immediate enrollment.

The tuition for their LPN program was $4,000, which I thought was surprisingly cheap, but the school had a lot of students so I guessed that Lafortune was making enough to pay his bills. I submitted a down payment of $3,000 and would pay the balance in installments.

Despite my hard-charging attitude, I soon discovered that the course was, as my former customer had warned, very hard. I had trouble keeping up with my course material, which to most of my fellow students was a review since they had experience as Certified Nurse Aides. Many were Haitian or from Latin America.

On my first exam, I received a 76 when 70 was passing. On top of my anxieties concerning my studies, I heard rumors from other students that the school was in trouble. When graduating students began applying for their nursing license, they discovered that the school was not accredited and therefore its courses didn't count. What we also learned was that as students in JLF University, we were actually enrolled in another school, one run by a business partner of Lafortune. Turned out Lafortune was lying to his partner about how many students were enrolled in the nursing program and pocketing the difference. Angered by this betrayal, the partner severed the ties between his school and JLF University.

We students began asking questions about the university as threats of legal action against Lafortune hovered in the air. He met with our classes to reassure us that the university and its nursing program remained on solid footing. As he explained himself, he paced in front of the class, looking spiffy and collected in his expensive suit and designer eyeglasses.

"Let me assure you," he said, his voice a lilting Haitian Creole accent. "Our school's placement of graduates in the state's licensing board is one of the highest in Florida. You all are new to this but I guarantee that JLF University has one of the best reputations of any nursing school."

But Lafortune's words were too slick, like he was hiding something. I looked about the classroom and saw that I wasn't the only one who still looked skeptical.

Lafortune must've sensed that as well, because at our next class session he brought a young woman he introduced as Paola Salvant, a recent graduate who he claimed had just passed the state LPN licensing exam. She was pretty and a little too done up in nice clothes to be considered a hard-working stiff like the rest of us, who slaved away at at least one job and attended class.

"The exam was a piece of cake," she said.

"What was the hardest question?" one of the other students asked.

"I'm afraid I'm not permitted to talk about the test," she replied.

"But you can tell us what subjects were presented," another student chimed in. "Like did they ask about hyperthyroidism?"

Paola blinked and her perfect smile turned flat. "Uh, like I said, I can't talk about the exam."

I smelled a rat, and it was her. I asked, "But you can tell us where you took the exam."

Her eyes cut to Lafortune's, and she shifted uncomfortably. "Uh, yes, it was at the hospital."

"What hospital?" I pressed.

Now even that smooth-talking Lafortune appeared off balance.

"I don't remember," Paola answered. "Someone drove me there. I was so concerned about the test that I wasn't paying attention."

"How much did the test cost?" I continued.

Paola again looked at Lafortune.

He cleared his throat and checked his watch. "I'm afraid Ms. Salvant is running late to another appointment."

Paola kept her eyes on the floor as she walked out the door, Lafortune close behind her. His attempt to settle our doubts had clearly backfired.

As the weeks passed, the rumors about the university's troubles kept gathering steam. Since I had invested so much of my time and money, I kept at my studies and hoped for the best.

One morning I arrived at the school and noticed a crowd of students at the front gate. I wondered why no one had gone inside, and as I approached, I overheard the students grumbling angrily. The front gate was padlocked.

One of them groused bitterly, "That damn Lafortune was lying to us all along. I hope they throw him in jail."

A Haitian student, a woman my age, threatened, "I'm going to use voodoo on him. He'll pay all right, for a long time."

I grasped the bars of the gate and gazed, stunned, at the university's building. *Why did Lafortune have to be a crook? Now what was I going to do?*

Someone let out a groan that spoke for all of us. "We've lost all our money."

I turned away from the gate and headed back to my car. I needed time to gather my thoughts and think of a plan.

In the aftermath, I learned that the Latin-American students had the resources to apply to legitimate, more expensive schools while the Haitians were left on their own. For my part, I was accepted in the LPN program at the Sigma Institute of Health. But the tuition was a whopping $11,000 for one year. With what I had saved, I could manage a down payment of $2,700 even though they wanted $3,500. But they let me start anyway.

As at JLF University, my lack of experience as a CNA really added to my course load. The instructors assumed I knew medical abbreviations such as PRN—as needed; NPO—nothing by mouth; BID—twice daily, and terms such as emesis basin, which was a vomit pan. On my own I had to learn how to insert a Foley catheter and use a Hoyer Lift, that hoisted a person from a bed and into a chair. I was committed to finishing this program as fast as I could, and that meant cramming two and a half years of course work into thirteen months. Needless to say, I was struggling.

On top of this, I managed to buy a home so I could bring my mother from Jamaica to live with me. The year was 2004. I was still working at The Check Cashing Store and they offered a second part-time gig of recording ads for a local radio program. For once, my Jamaican accent worked to my advantage, as people listening to my voice knew that I was from their community. But even with this extra work, money remained tight.

At the supermarket I noticed a homemade flyer advertising for a live-in caretaker to assist an elderly person. I tore loose one of the phone number tabs, as I had a friend named Courtney who was out of a job and so I referred the listing to him.

The next day he called. "Petergay, thanks for the offer but it didn't pan out. They want a woman for the position."

Mother was looking for work so I asked if she wanted the job.

"I don't know anything about caring for the elderly," she replied.

"They pay five hundred a week. What would it cost you to ask?"

Mother thought it over and agreed. We did the interview in my home and she got the job despite her lack of experience. Mother was like me in that once we can talk to you one-on-one, we could probably talk you into doing what we wanted. I shuttled her to and from work and deposited her checks in the bank.

However, mother's new job didn't alleviate the pressure building on me to pay for the LPN program. I started thinking about her money sitting unused in the bank. So I came up with a plan. I convinced myself that it was okay if I borrowed her money with the promise that I'd pay it back as soon as I started working as a nurse.

After months of hard work, I finally got my LPN certificate, but something kept me from proceeding with the state exam. It turned out I was afraid of blood. I'd freeze up anytime I had to take blood or administer an injection or an IV. The sight of blood made me queasy and filled me with dread.

A friend, Ian Swaby, noticed that I was still working at my check-cashing job.

"Petergay," he asked, "didn't you get your LPN?"

"I did," I answered proudly.

"Then why are you still working here?"

I didn't reply right away and when I finally did, I said, "I'm still sorting some things out."

"What's to sort out? I'll tell you what's the real issue. You've gotten too comfortable working here. You lost your ambition."

The truth stung. Yes, if I had worked so hard at getting my LPN, why was I wasting all that sacrifice by not getting a job as a nurse?

But before I could move on that, my troubles got worse.

Sandra Morgan, one of my fellow students at JLF University, stopped by to cash a check for $1,032. She explained it came from the sale of her home. Since I knew Sandra personally, without hesitation I gave her the money.

That night the check bounced because of a stop payment.

When I heard this the next morning, my heart sank. Both of us were in trouble. I called her husband David and asked what was going on. Turns out Sandra and David were having marital troubles, and the sale of their house was part of the divorce settlement.

"Sandra told me nothing about the check from the sale of the house," he explained. "So when I learned about that check, I put a stop payment on it."

"But I already gave the money to Sandra."

"You'll have to talk to her."

I called Sandra right away.

"Oh, I'm so sorry, Petergay," she said. "There was a misunderstanding between David and me about this. I'll be there this afternoon and make good on the check."

I hung up the phone, warm with the reassurance that I had not misjudged my friend.

At an hour before closing I started watching the clock as I waited for her to arrive. Minute by minute, I could feel a noose tighten around my neck. Then at closing time, I called her.

"Please forgive me, Petergay," she lamented. "But I had problems with my car, and you know this rush-hour traffic. I'll be there first thing tomorrow, I promise."

And the next morning, she burned me again.

That afternoon the corporate office called me directly. They wanted details about what had happened, and I told them the truth. They arranged for a meeting with the manager, a rep from corporate, and me.

The manager greeted me with solemn looks when I reported in. She led me to a small table in her office where the rep from corporate waited. Heart beating frantically, I took a seat. The mood was grim and much like that of a police interrogation.

The rep was a humorless blond-haired man with an expression as gray as his suit. He opened my file and pointed to the forms I'd signed before I was allowed to work. He began, "Your signature on the forms acknowledges that you are aware of the rules regarding cashing checks. Yes?"

"Yes," I answered, nodding.

He pointed to a section highlighted in yellow. "Specifically, that a check in the amount written by Sandra Morgan should've been cleared before you gave her cash."

"I know that," I replied.

"But you gave her the money anyway. Why?"

"Because she was my friend. I thought I could trust her."

The rep turned the file so I could read it. "Show me where it says you can cash checks for friends without waiting for them to clear."

"I'm sorry, I made a mistake."

He gazed at the manager.

Taking her cue, she said, "From where we see this, it appears that you colluded with Morgan."

"No, that's not true. Like I said, I made a mistake. I cashed a bad check, yes, that was my fault. But Sandra knew it was bad. She's promised me twice that she would pay it back, but she skipped out on you and me both."

The manager sighed. "We could press charges against you."

My breath froze.

The rep added, "But collusion would be difficult to prove in court."

At that, the manager announced, "Petergay, you're dismissed. Immediately."

In plain English, I was fired.

Yes, I felt bad for what had happened to me and that someone I trusted had betrayed me. But I had bills to pay so I couldn't waste time wallowing in pity. I hustled out and applied at United Check Cashing. I told the manager everything about what had happened with Sandra Morgan, and that I had learned a bitter and lasting lesson from that experience. They seemed pleased with my attitude and offered me a job.

At last I breathed in relief. I felt like I'd dodged a huge oncoming boulder, and that this reprieve from tribulation was my wake-up call. My mind was made up. I would take the LPN exam and move forward.

The trouble was, months had passed since I'd finished school. As a result, I failed the exam.

# CHAPTER 16

Although failing the LPN licensing exam was a huge blow, it did have the benefit of making me think hard about my life. While in the nursing school, I'd applied myself and received perfect marks. Then after graduation, an ambivalence set in. I was at one of those moments when you work hard toward a goal, and once you reach it, you're afraid of the change it represents and become reluctant to take the next step forward. In waiting six months to take the licensing exam—and thinking that because I'd done well in school I therefore didn't need to study—I ended up forgetting a lot and losing ground that I had labored so hard to achieve. Big mistake on my part.

I was at home planning what to do next when Mother brought up, "Ricardo is not doing well. He's in bad shape."

The announcement shocked me. Certainly, my father and I had never been on good terms, but he did figure prominently in my life and was part of my family.

Then Mother dropped the bombshell. "I want to see him before it's too late."

I panicked. If she tapped into her savings account to buy her ticket to Jamaica, she'd see that her money was missing. I had to repay what I'd secretly borrowed and soon, and I couldn't do it with what I earned at the check-cashing store. Now I was under tremendous pressure to make things right before she discovered that I had taken from her money. Ironically, I'd done so to pay for my LPN schooling and now I was in a serious jam for dragging my feet about getting a nursing license.

To cover what I'd done, I had to knuckle down. I pulled out my LPN course materials and after work, I studied in the local Barnes & Noble from 5:00 PM to closing time every night. The effort was arduous, but it was my own fault for not taking the licensing exam while the material was still fresh in my mind. I could hear the clock ticking down to disaster, and I feared I couldn't pass the exam, find a well-paying nursing job, and replenish Mother's bank account before it was too late.

Fortunately, this time, I passed the licensing exam. Now to get the right nursing job. While in school I did clinical rotations where I spent several days getting exposed to various areas of the nursing field. Working as a hospital nurse seemed too impersonal. I dreaded working home nursing care because those situations were so depressing.

Interestingly, it was hospice that drew me in. Prior to this I was afraid of dying and death, but what happened during my rotation dramatically changed my mind. I was assigned a 91-year-old Cuban woman named Miriam Gonzales. The other nurses were rough with her and spent so much time on their computers that they couldn't be otherwise bothered. I asked my instructor if I could attend to Miriam and practice my Spanish. I had learned some during my stay in Miami and wanted to build on what I already knew. Sitting beside the bed, I took her hand. It was light and fragile and like holding a tiny bird.

She turned to me. *"Hablas español?"*

*"Hablo un poco,"* I replied, *"pero entiendo mucho."*

We managed to communicate enough for me to understand her concerns and fears. She had come from Cuba with her one daughter and spent all her money on her. Now that Miriam was old and infirm, her daughter had placed her in a nursing home and now in hospice. But the daughter was too busy to visit, and Miriam was terrified she would die alone and forgotten like a lost dog. I did my best to comfort her and express my sincere care for her condition.

When I returned to the school I told the staff that I wanted to be assigned to watch over Miriam. But when I arrived back at the nursing home I was told she had passed away that morning. The news devastated me. She had died alone and probably soiled herself with no one to clean her up right away. This episode drove home the importance of good hospice care. I could let my patients live out the last of their time on earth with someone who genuinely cared and allowed them to die with dignity. By working in hospice, I was convinced I could make a difference.

Soon after I'd received my nursing license, one of my Jamaican friends, Ian, stopped by United Check Cashing to see what I was up to. "Still here, Petergay? Looks like you're wanting to make a career of check cashing."

"That's not true. I am looking for a nursing job."

"In that case," Ian said, "I can give you a referral to a nurse employment agency."

He gave me the details and I applied that day. Since they had several openings in hospice care I was hired right away.

It was at this job where I encountered my first dead body as a nurse. I'd left my patient in his room, and when I returned, he had died. I got so freaked out that I called my mother. During the conversation, as she talked me down, she opened up more about my father's past. She explained the reason years back about when he'd been fired as the director of Bailey's Funeral Home. Seems he'd gotten drunk (no surprise there) and switched bodies that were to be interred. Needless to say, this mistake greatly embarrassed the funeral home, and my father was promptly fired. That episode was another incident in a life marred by bad decisions and his refusal to deal with being an alcoholic. But that didn't explain why he took out his frustrations and failures on me.

Mother had given me much to think about regarding my life and my responsibilities. After stepping through the procedures of dealing with that particular dead body, I remained at the job and worked for ten days straight. I deposited every hard-earned penny into Mother's account.

With the money situation squared away, Mother and I traveled to Jamaica. My father was 62 years old and quite sick, too frail in fact to talk much. What I wanted from him was an explanation as to why he'd been so cruel to me as a child. Despite his abuse, I was back at his side as a dutiful daughter, paying for his medical care and for a second opinion from another doctor to make sure he was getting the necessary treatment. But my efforts didn't do much to coax what I wanted from him.

He lay in his bed, baggy clothes swaddling his thin frame so he looked like a scarecrow in repose. Ironically, I relied on my training in hospice to guide me on how to handle this situation. Holding his hand or stroking his arm, I'd talk. I recalled all the times I'd recoiled from him in fear and disgust, and now I desperately wanted him to open up and share what was on his mind. But his rheumy eyes wouldn't focus on me.

The few times he spoke, he babbled incoherently and never recognized Mother or me. Dementia had short-circuited his mind and my queries to him went unanswered. It was like talking to a statue.

Certain there was nothing more we could do for him other than wait for the end, Mother and I returned to Florida. Once there, I worked two jobs, back-to-back. I slept when I could between shifts or when my patients and their families were themselves asleep. I changed clothes in my car. The ordeal was brutal, but I needed to earn and save as much money as I could. You could say that much of this stress was self-imposed. You could ask, Petergay, why did you put yourself through so much anguish? Others in your family didn't make such efforts, so why should you?

I guess it had to do with my sense of never seeing myself as being adequate enough and so constantly disappointing others. I still carried the burden from childhood of constantly being rebuked and punished. I had a lot to prove to the world, and so challenged myself to make extraordinary efforts because I felt I had no other choice. I wanted to be acknowledged as a good person. Guilt forced me to at last confess to my mother that I'd taken her money.

My words didn't come easily for I was admitting treachery against someone who trusted me deeply. I waited for a calm moment at home. "Mother, I have something to tell you."

She guessed by the strained undertone in my voice that I had dramatic news to share.

"Mother, I've been taking money from your savings account."

My breath clotted in my throat as I had no idea how she would react. Incredibly, Mother looked at me with an expression that fluctuated between pity and admiration. "You could've asked me for the money."

"I couldn't. If I did, it would've been like I had let you down."

"How so, Petergay?"

"Because I wasn't making enough to cover all our expenses."

She took my hands. "But you did. And you replaced all the money you've taken, right?"

"Yes."

"So, no harm done."

"Then you forgive me, Mother?"

"There's nothing to forgive. You've done more for me than anyone else in our family."

Leave it to Mother to tell me what I needed to hear.

On December 7, 2006, we received the inevitable call. My father finally passed on. Mother returned to Jamaica on the 11th. I stayed behind to keep working and finally joined her on the 19th. While my father had died without either of us having the opportunity to mend our relationship, I did get some vindication on another personal matter.

My friend Verona remained close to my family and she came by to offer emotional support during my father's funeral. As I made arrangements to pay for the funeral, she took me aside.

"Petergay, I have something to discuss. Remember years ago, when you stayed at my house?"

I did, and it remained an incident that I didn't want to talk about. I wanted to work on my father's funeral arrangements instead of dredging up uncomfortable memories from my past. What she referred to was when her husband Raulston tried to force himself on me. When I refused his advances, he accused me of being a thief and turned Verona against me.

"I was wrong about you," she said. "I should've believed what you told me about Raulston."

"It happened long ago," I replied. "I've moved on."

"I wish I could say that," Verona said. "After you left, Raulston kept at his lecherous ways. We had a cousin stay with us and he molested her."

"That's terrible," I replied, not certain what I should say. I gasped, "Oh dear." Now, regrettably, the worm had turned, and Verona's failure to address her husband's predatory desires had brought disastrous consequences.

"So you see, Petergay. You were right about Raulston all along. Had I listened to you then, I would've saved myself a lot of heartache."

"I appreciate you sharing this, Verona." But I felt no satisfaction. No one deserved the anguish Raulston was putting her through.

"I'm so sorry." Her eyes misted. "Please say that you forgive me."

I was hoping for some closure with my past and Verona brought it. This was a brave step on her part, and I wondered how many others on the island would offer an apology for what they'd done to me. But as I'd said, I had moved on.

"Verona, of course I forgive you."

We hugged and her warm tears stained my neck.

Later that day, my friend Sandra approached and admitted she had a confession as well. When Verona had asked that I leave her house, she had given me a letter to pass along to my half-sister Karen. Since I didn't want to go home, I handed the letter to Sandra to deliver for me. What I didn't know at the time was that Verona had enclosed $150. When Karen received the letter, the money was missing and I was blamed.

Sandra explained, "I stole that money, Petergay. And when

everyone was calling you a thief, I joined in, knowing that it was me who was the real crook." She broke down in sobs.

At the time years ago, I figured as much. Now it was water under the bridge and until Sandra brought it up, the episode was long forgotten.

I pondered the reason for these confessions. Maybe it was my father's dying and the reckoning that comes with the inevitable that awaits all of us that moved people to make amends for their transgressions.

We laid my father to rest on December 21. So much between us had been left both undone and unsaid. His passing created a void in me that I knew would remain empty. Not that I missed him, but now I'd never know why he mistreated like he had.

Relatives from all over Jamaica came to my father's funeral. Since my childhood, much gossip had been spread about me, so people knew who I was. Petergay Dunkley, the unwed teenage mother and homeless girl, the one who once danced at a go-go club, was now a nurse in America and making good money. While everyone else stayed behind and did little to improve their circumstances, other than try shortcuts and avoid the hard work necessary to escape their poverty, I bore down and exploited every opportunity that came my way. The unseemly anecdotes about me were now outshone by my accomplishments, and people who once looked down their nose at me now wanted favors.

My cousin Delores was typical. Soon after the funeral, she stepped close. "Petergay, it's so good to see you. I've missed you a lot."

Which was a lie. If anything, what Delores missed was saying bad things behind my back.

"You've done so well in America. Of anyone that I knew who could succeed, I knew it would be you."

Another big lie. When I was homeless, Delores used to call me street trash, and say that I'd never amount to anything.

"You know what makes us Jamaicans such a proud people?" she continued. "It's the way they take care of each other."

Her insincere tone lit a fuse in me. "What do you need?"

"If you could lend me fifty dollars, I could buy a new dress and shoes. I could make myself look more presentable when I apply for a new job."

If Delores did buy new clothes, it would be to attract new boyfriends. I kept my anger in check and answered, "Once I get the funeral costs settled, I might be able to help." I planned to be off the island by then.

As each relative or acquaintance hit me up for money or a favor, my resentment continued to build. When I was down and out and needed help, they chased me off like a beggar scrounging for scraps. Now they acted as if there had never been any bad feelings between us.

My obligation as a Christian woman would've been to forgive and forget. But I wasn't that strong or magnanimous.

My father's passing and my relatives using that occasion to flock around me like hungry vultures put me in a deep funk. So, when my sister Donnet invited me to a Christmas party, I only reluctantly went along. I wasn't overcome with much holiday cheer. But it was at this party that I found the kind of sweet love that was missing from my life.

# CHAPTER 17

The Christmas season, 2006. I wasn't in any mood to celebrate. We had only recently buried my father, and his passing left many unanswered questions about our relationship that would bother me for the rest of my life.

On top of that, friends, but mostly family members who used to talk behind my back and lament what a loser I was—and now that I was living in America, working as a nurse and doing well—were hitting me up nonstop for money.

At this Christmas party, I sat with Donnet, and she did her best to cheer me up. We were dressed in our best party clothes, and once surrounded by festive music and people having a good time, I started to loosen up and let my resentments go. I had brought along Phillipa and my sister-in-law Melanie. Phillipa and I were checking the men out.

I joked with her, "I don't know why Donnet invited me to this party. There aren't any decent guys here."

No sooner had I said that, when one of the guests appeared from around the corner, and he immediately caught my attention. Not only was he handsome, he also moved with a confident yet warm manner that beckoned me to know him better. We made eye contact and immediately started laughing. It was as if we had both been thinking the same thought—that there isn't a decent person to hook up with and suddenly, we see each other.

He approached our group. "Would any of you like a drink?"

Since I rarely drank alcohol, I replied, "Water."

Melanie and Phillipa asked for some of the spiked punch. He turned about and returned with our refreshments, then left, my interest in him following like a wake behind a boat.

"Who is he?" I asked.

"His name is Jamian," Donnet answered. "But everyone knows him as Jay."

"How do you know?"

"He's my friend's nephew."

Jay had gone to the next room, where I could see him in a circle talking with others. "Let's get him to sit with us."

"How are we going to do that?" Phillipa asked.

"Simple," I replied. "We'll walk up to him. You take one hand and I'll take the other and we'll bring him back here."

We did just that. Jay could hardly have been more surprised by the gesture, but he handled it well. He accompanied us, grinning, delighted by the attention. He and I chatted, engaging in an easy conversation about what we had in common and where we grew up on the island. He was from Pepper and I was from Santa Cruz. What weighed on my mind was that for the last several days, every time I revealed I was from the U.S., people hit me up for money. Because of that, I had gotten into the habit of not mentioning where I now lived.

As the party wound down, Jay asked if I wanted to go to another party in Black River. He was kind and honest and charming, so different than the other men I'd run into during my life. Though I wanted to say yes, my experiences with men kept me guarded and withdrawn.

"Call me later." I gave him my brother's phone number. But as I did that, I got so nervous about what I was getting into that I excused myself and disappeared down the hall, where I locked myself in a bathroom. I felt silly and immature about what I was doing, but my fear over getting hurt and humiliated again made me hide.

The next day, Donnet arrived at my mother's house to tell me, "Jay called and was asking about you. He didn't realize you and I are related."

Anticipation swept through me. "What did he want?"

"He was very smitten by you," Donnet said. "He told me that he'd finally met the woman he wants to marry."

Hearing that only amped up my anxiety. Though Jay seemed like a great catch, I hardly knew him. I kept second-guessing myself about his intentions and avoided him up to the time I returned to the U.S. When Donnet called me to ask for $50 American, she added that Jay had stopped by her house several times. She said, "He's figured out that you and I are half-sisters."

I was as curious about him as he was about me. "Get his phone number."

"What about the fifty dollars?" she insisted.

"I'll wire you the money, but get me his number and then I'll give you the control number so Western Union will release the money to you."

"All right."

The next day she called with Jay's phone number. Hesitantly, I called. Although I had survived a lot of dangerous episodes— fighting with my ex-husband, time in jail, stabbing another man who tried to fondle me—as I waited for Jay to pick up the phone, I still had the flutters like a young schoolgirl.

"Hello," he answered.

"Hey there, Jay. It's me. Petergay Dunkley." I was so nervous that my palms were sweating.

"Where are you calling from?" he asked. "I don't recognize the caller ID."

"I'm calling from Fort Lauderdale."

"Where's that?"

"It's in Florida. The U.S."

The line on his end went quiet.

"You there?" I asked.

"Yeah, I'm here." His tone grew sharp. "Why didn't you tell me you were from America?"

I wanted to explain that I didn't want to because in Jamaica, as soon as you tell someone you're from America, they assume you have money and start angling to get it. It's not that I thought Jay was like that, but keeping tight-lipped regarding details about myself was a defensive habit.

"It's that—"

"I thought you were different," he interrupted. "Instead, you're just like everyone else around here. Always lying."

"I wasn't lying, listen, let me explain."

"No," he countered. "Before I talk to you again, let me think about this. We'll talk then."

With that, he hung up.

I held my phone, feeling hollow. This was our second conversation and all that occurred was that we had no good reason to continue. It seemed no matter what I did, and no matter how noble my intentions, the situation always blew up in my face. But I hadn't lost hope in Jay. I was certain that once I talked to him again I could clear up this misunderstanding. For now, I had to let the matter rest.

On the home front, I decided to expand my social circle, and did so by joining the Faith Apostolic Church. Growing up in Jamaica, I never went to church much. But in Fort Lauderdale, this assembly offered an appealing blend of camaraderie with fellow Jamaicans and a religious message that proved inspirational and encouraging amid the chaos of Florida life. The congregation welcomed me and it was a place I could go to for comfort and reassurance. And to show just how small the world could be, the head of the church, Pastor Douglas, was a cousin of my father. Certain that I had found sanctuary, I immersed myself in church activities and volunteered as an assistant secretary and to do radio promotions. One of the more highly regarded men of the congregation was Michael, who also served as a lay-minister and became my spiritual mentor.

But like anything else, belonging to this church was a compromise. This denomination was both socially and politically conservative. Pastor Douglas preached that the end times were near and we needed to prepare ourselves for the final reckoning with our Creator. He emphasized that the Bible presented everything we needed to know about life, and so he saw no need for anyone in his congregation to pursue higher education. Moreover, learning the wrong thing could cause you to question the Bible and the authority of the church.

I, on the other hand, credited my college studies as instrumental in my success. I couldn't understand Pastor Douglas' attitude since the better educated his congregation became, the better jobs they could get, and in turn would be able to tithe more, which benefited his ministry. But I kept these thoughts to myself.

Despite these contrary opinions, I embraced the church and its teachings, applying myself to live according to Scripture. Michael baptized me, and with that act, I became a full-fledged member of the congregation.

While I remained committed to the church, my independent spirit kept getting me the wrong kind of attention, especially as the church was tight-knit to the point of being cliquish and we tended to be suspicious of anyone from outside our assembly. Everyone was expected to dress up for Sunday worship service, and this was a time to flaunt our fanciest clothing. But in keeping with our conservative outlook, makeup was forbidden.

One Sunday morning, as I was filing into the chapel, Donna, the pastor's wife, took me aside.

"Petergay, where is your hat?"

"I'm not used to wearing a hat and don't own one."

She frowned. "Remember what it says in 1st Corinthians about the shame of a woman not covering her head?" Donna was quick to quote Scripture when it served her purpose.

"All right," I acceded.

Her gaze dropped to my legs. "And your dress is too short."

I'd had enough of her condescending attitude. "What does it matter? Long skirts don't hide sin."

Lips pursing in disapproval, she stepped away. "Very well, just don't forget that the Lord is watching, and you'll have to answer to Him."

I had a different perspective on my relationship with God, one that was more positive. Thanks to my LPN credentials, I was on my feet financially. In fact, I was doing better than I imagined possible when I arrived in America. In light of that, I decided to reward myself with my dream car, a new Mercedes sedan, in black.

This roomy automobile allowed me to bring prospective members to the church, and in this way, I strived to be a better person. But not everyone else saw it that way. By now I realized that everything that I didn't like about the Jamaican community was distilled in this church: the gossip mongering, the petty squabbling over status, and the constant judging over trivial matters.

When I brought prospective church members in my new car, I overheard, "That Petergay, just because she's making decent money as a nurse, she thinks she's too good to drive a Toyota like the rest of us."

Donna never let an opportunity slip by to remind me of my place. Like the time I brought a woman who was covered in piercings and tattoos to worship service. No sooner had I ushered her into the church than Donna pulled me aside.

"Petergay, what are you doing bringing someone like her to our church?"

The question confused me. "What do you mean, someone like her? Doesn't the Bible say we have to be 'fishers of men'?"

Donna skewered me with a very unchristian-like glare. "You know your problem? You're too stubborn. You always have to do things your way."

Frankly, I was proud of my stubbornness. It had gotten me where I was today.

I was making enough money that I decided to invest in real estate. Unfortunately, my timing was off. This was in late 2007, and the U.S. was sliding toward a recession.

Something else happened that year. I learned that Allen's drug habits had caught up to him. On June 30, in Washington some teenagers found him on the roof of a house, dead from an overdose. I felt sad that he could never overcome his demons, but his choices were his alone.

Back in Florida, real estate prices were ridiculously expensive, and as high as they were, the prevailing wisdom was to buy something before the price went up even further. I bought a quarter-acre lot in Lehigh Acres for $9,500, and a builder convinced to me to buy another acre and a quarter for $40,000. Then in 2008, when the recession tore through the national economy, real estate prices hit bottom, but I hung on to my properties.

In the meantime, Jay and I smoothed things out, and I flew to Jamaica and back once a month. We took our time nurturing this relationship. I made him understand why I'd been evasive in my first dealings with him. For my part, I learned that Jay was 22 compared to my 30, but that difference in age didn't bother either one of us as we became engaged.

Seeing how gossip traveled between Jamaicans faster than electricity through wires, it didn't take long for word to reach the church that I was getting hitched to a younger man, and immediately, tongues started to wag.

Donna led the pack. "Petergay, I thought you were smarter than this, marrying such a younger man. All he wants is a green card, and once he gets here, he'll leave you right away. You can't trust these Jamaicans, always scheming to take advantage of you. Besides, you never get it right with men. First you marry an older man and that was a disaster. Now you're marrying a younger man, and for some reason you think it's not going to end the same way."

I had been hearing the same thing during my trips back to Jamaica, and all this negative talk filled me with doubt. Since my sister Donnet had introduced me to Jay, I asked her opinion.

"Jay is a great guy," she reassured me. "He's a good man."

When I returned to Florida, during a work break I discussed my worries with Mary, an older LPN that I shared assignments with. She was sitting in a chair, enjoying a cup of coffee. "Where's your fiancé from?"

"Goshen," I answered.

"I'm from Goshen," Mary replied, surprised. "What's his name?"

"Jay. Jamian."

"Jamian?" Mary exclaimed, and she rose from her chair. "Deslyn Jones' son?"

"I think so."

"I was there the night he was born. As twins. He's a good, good man."

Mary's words soothed me, and confirmed how I felt about Jay and that I wasn't making a big mistake in marrying him.

We exchanged nuptials on March 29, 2008, in Mandeville, Jamaica. Because of all the unflattering things some in my family and friends had been saying about me, I decided not to invite them to my wedding. In our culture, people hear you're getting married they just show up anyway. And when they do show up, they want you to buy the nice clothes for the occasion, so I kept the time and place as secret as I could. Not long ago these same acquaintances were hitting me up for money, but they didn't hesitate in using my marriage to a younger man as a reason to smear me with malicious rumors. They kept reminding me that I was an outcast, that I'd been the only one in the family to get pregnant as a teen, that I'd married a white man who proved to be a druggie. They argued that in marrying a standup guy like Jay I was only trying to get right with my past.

In July 2009, Jay finally joined me in Fort Lauderdale. I told him I was planning to leave the city and in the meantime, he had a month to get situated. While I was happy that Jay was here, Mother remained skeptical of him and our marriage. However, her opinion changed when she had a chance to talk with him.

This happened when I mentioned, "I want to send a present to someone I know in Goshen."

Mother replied, "I too have a friend in Goshen. He's in bad shape and just had his second leg removed."

I said, "The guy I know is also a double-amputee."

Mother looked astonished. "Then, Jamian is his grandson. So his family are good friends with my mother and grandfather."

Now that Mother knew who Jay was, she started correcting the rumors floating about the church regarding Jay and me.

For his part, Jay needed to find work. He wasn't interested in real estate and stated an interest in driving commercial trucks. I sold my house in Fort Lauderdale on a short sale before I was underwater with the mortgage, and we moved into a duplex.

I job-hopped from a position in Lehigh Acres to a better one at Hope Hospice in Fort Myers. We rented a one-room efficiency and put all our belongings in storage. At first, we slept on the floor until we bought an air mattress. One morning, while I was taking a shower, Jay tried to iron my blouse on the mattress and popped it. Soon afterwards we moved into a house with larger accommodations.

As the months passed, the gossip in church quieted. I thought my situation there was okay, until something happened that knocked the props from under me and made me realize I had to accelerate my plans to leave Fort Lauderdale for good. I was remodeling my home by adding a second bedroom that I could sublet. Since Michael worked as a contractor, I hired him to do the addition.

I thought I knew him well, and I felt comfortable being alone with him. Aside from Pastor Douglas, there wasn't a more Godly man in the congregation, or so I thought.

One afternoon he stopped by to measure and prepare an estimate. "Petergay," he said, "would you like to go on a cruise of the Caribbean?"

The idea of a vacation on a big fancy ship sounded appealing.

"I'd love to go. Let me get with your wife and discuss our schedules."

"Oh, she's not going."

The feeling of ice water ran through my veins. There was so much wrong in his proposition. One, he was married and coming on to me, another member of the church. Plus, Michael very well knew that I was married. He was so brazen about this adultery that he was willing to take off right under his wife's nose.

My faith in the church was shaken. In one sense, Michael had represented everything positive that I admired about the church, and now he'd turned my perceptions upside down.

I shared my concerns in private with Pastor Douglas. He in turn, shared them with his wife Donna, who in turn tattle-taled about me to the church secretary. She then called me right away.

"Petergay, what's this about you and Michael?"

By this time, I'd learned that she and Michael were having an affair, and she was calling me in a fit of jealousy.

This episode finally ended my interest in the church. I had hoped for a supportive community and instead I find one that was pious, judgmental, and supremely hypocritical.

Jay was likewise done with the church and the local Jamaican community. Yes, we could be very tight and supportive. But taken to extremes like now, we clung to one another and wallowed in our shortcomings rather than finding a way forward.

Our situation is best illustrated by the fable, "Crabs in a Bucket."

A man sees another man fishing for crabs off a pier. The first man notices that when the other man pulls a crab out of the water, he places it in one of two buckets. One bucket is open and the other is covered with a board.

The man asks, "Why is one bucket open and the other has a board?"

The second man explains, "That's because the bucket with the board is filled with Chinese crabs and the open one has Jamaican crabs."

"So?"

The second man continues, "I have to cover the Chinese crabs because they'll help each other try to escape."

"And the Jamaican crabs?"

"I don't worry about them. As soon as they see another one trying to climb out, the others will drag him back down."

Jay and I were done being crabs in this bucket. In 2009, we quit the church and moved to Fort Myers in search of new opportunities.

# CHAPTER 18

As I considered this change in my life, I reflected back to my experience with Miriam Gonzales. I remained troubled by what had happened to her. In her last days, she and I had made a connection, and it was through this bond that I realized just how important hospice work was. Every human life, no matter how beautiful and blessed, ended in tragedy. We all die, that's an inescapable fact of our existence.

In death, we don't have many options about the way we transition from this world to the next. The options are to die suddenly without having the opportunity to make peace with ourselves and our loved ones, or to face death for a time and be allowed the opportunity to take stock of one's life. The first means that we go without much pain or lingering anguish. But when people die like that, it leaves a void in their immediate community and a heartache that often is never healed.

Regardless, unless we choose suicide, the choice is not up to us. We humans are like every other creature God created. Foremost in our DNA is the will to survive, to hang on for just one more day.

Looking back upon my life, my experience with tragedy and pain prepared me to pursue a career in hospice care. We provide the last experience for our patients and in that regard, we must connect in a way that is spiritual and comforting. Those outside the profession think it must be sad for us to see people die all the time. But the truth is that hospice makes the difference between dying miserably and dying in peace. We don't just care for the patients but also for the families. Hospice is better than dying of neglect in a hospital or at home. What we provide is not about death, but about living one's final hours to their fullest and with dignity.

While I enjoyed being in the continuous hospice care field as an LPN, I decided that I could better serve my patients if I became an RN. Also, I'd get an appreciated bump in salary and that money would allow me to get back into real estate. The move to Fort Myers pulled Jamian and me away from the claustrophobic environment of Lauderdale, but thinking long term, we decided it was best to sink roots in Georgia. With that in mind we visited the Atlanta area and discovered that the market for LPNs was really tight. However, RNs were in high demand.

Returning to Fort Myers, I enrolled in Florida Southwestern State College and began taking the entrance exams and prerequisites for their RN program. One obstacle was the waiting list of 400 candidates for a mere 25 openings. What would help my chances was that I qualified for the bridge program from LPN to RN. But the circumstance that ultimately determined my place in line would be the prerequisites I'd taken and my score on the Health Educational Systems Inc. (HESI) exam.

I took the exam and scored 94. The following week I was told that I was accepted into the program. That was in August 2012. As if I didn't have enough stress working full time and studying for the RN program, I learned that I was pregnant.

I graduated in November 2013 and promptly took the state

licensing board exam, which I passed on February 11, 2014. Though I was ready to leave Florida, Jamian and I stayed until after I gave birth. In July 2014, we had a daughter, Jhevonia.

In June 2015, we moved to Atlanta and I started interviewing. Right away I received two job offers and I accepted the position as a case manager with Amedisys Hospice. But I didn't fit into the environment and left after three weeks. From there I worked as a charge nurse and Patient Care Coordinator at Hospice Atlanta. That position didn't last long either before I accepted a job as Assistant Director of Nursing at Pruitthealth Hospice in Norcross, Georgia.

I had by this time in my life reached a level of material comfort and financial stability that I hadn't dreamed possible when I was a homeless, unwed teenage mother back in Jamaica.

My career in hospice has allowed me to evaluate my life, and what I've learned from observing people in the last days among us has given me an enlightened perspective on what is and is not important.

On the surface, I've learned much about the technical aspects of the medical field. I've also learned how to deal with people. But the most valuable lessons I've taken to heart are those I learned from my hospice patients.

Foremost, I've appreciated that ultimately, friends and family are what life is about. It is these relationships that sustain and buoy you from cradle to the end.

In taking care of my patients, I learned not to judge since I'm not privy to all the details of what brought them to my care. Many of the patients and their families have life stories similar to mine. As people wait for the end, patients confide in you to unburden themselves—as is said, confession is good for the soul—or because they don't want their secrets to disappear when they die.

Families and loved ones also share intimate details. You learn that you're not always getting all the facts and that what is presented is often only one opinion. Consequently, I've learned not to take sides.

In the case of one patient, I overheard many of his family complain that he had been careless with his money to the point that it estranged him from many of his loved ones. Then in his last days, a dozen strangers arrived at the care center to pay their respects to him. It turns out that the money his family had accused him of wasting, he had actually spent to rescue three hundred refugees from the direst of circumstances in the Middle East. And he did so in secret as he wanted no praise for doing his humanitarian duty. These strangers shared tearful anecdotes that, had it not been for the unselfish generosity of this humble man, they and their families would've been wiped out. So, the epitaph for this man was not that of a wastrel but of a hero.

Some stories illustrate how bad outcomes can result from simple events. One of my patients was a young woman dying of AIDS. What happened was that she had too much to drink one night, and while inebriated was injected with a drug she became addicted to. Later, she contracted HIV from a shared needle and now here she was.

Others were tragically bizarre, like the woman who kept her dying husband in home hospice to steal his pain medications. She was found out when another of my nurses and I visited the home to check on his care. The poor man had been locked in the basement and lived in absolute neglect and was covered in filth. Needless to say, I called the police and had the husband transferred to a hospice facility to receive the care that he needed.

Some stories turn on cruel twists of fate. One attractive and very sweet woman in her early fifties was dying of a rare type of vaginal cancer. What made her condition pointedly ironic was that she and her husband had been swingers. You couldn't help but think that in some way she was being punished for her lifestyle, though I know God does not work that way. It was as if her vagina was rotting and from it gushed a dark brown and foul-smelling discharge. I put coffee grounds and rose water in her bandages to mask the odor. She was in excruciating pain and I gave her the maximum dose of morphine. Even so, she was aware of everything that was happening to her. When I cleaned her up, she would tell me, "I apologize for putting you through this."

We don't let animals suffer as she did. Every day I prayed that when I showed up, she'd be gone. She lasted for three long, miserable weeks before she finally expired. At least we had let her die with a measure of dignity.

Another time we had a 32-year-old woman die in our care from a brain aneurysm. What happened was that her husband had a baby with another woman. Our patient decided to get even by having an affair of her own. But during intercourse she suffered a stroke that turned fatal.

One time I found myself in a difficult situation with a patient who had been very abusive to his wife. This patient had pancreatic cancer and needed medication for his pain and diarrhea. After he was transferred to our unit, he became increasingly abusive with us, usually verbally, though once when I tried to give him his medicine, he grabbed and twisted my arm. I told him, "Sir, you're hurting me."

His eyes simmered with sadistic delight.

I tried prying his thumb loose but he was very strong. What complicated the situation for me was that I was responsible for giving him his drugs, and he wouldn't let me. Our staff doctor told me to summon him when the patient needed medication. Though this was my job, I couldn't take the slight personally.

Besides his abusive personality, this patient was angry at the world and scared of dying. Fortunately, he only remained with us for four days.

In another twist of irony, we had a patient whose father had died in our facility five years prior. His son told him that he was so impressed with the quality of our care, that when it was his time to go, he wanted to come to us. Then the son was brought in with rectal cancer.

We've had convicts transferred from prison who were dying from a variety of ailments such as cancer, HIV, and hepatitis. One of them was 82 years old, also suffering from rectal cancer, and was imprisoned for child molestation. He was brought to us under house arrest and wore an ankle bracelet. The victim's family waited for an apology but he gave none. He walked into our facility and passed quickly.

Another of these patients was an incarcerated murderer with cancer. He was especially dangerous. When one of our nurses wanted to give him drugs, he tried punching her. After that, the doctor had to keep him sedated. He was with us a week.

A meth addict was brought in, and he died from Hepatitis-C.

However, not all patients were dying from disease. One man was brought in with a brain injury from a fall and was brain dead when we got him.

Among the most memorable and poignant stories was the daughter who called from New Jersey to ask about her dying mother. Shortly thereafter, the daughter arrived at the facility but would not visit her mother, despite the tearful pleas.

The daughter explained her mother had done things to her that she could never forgive. When the daughter was eight years old, her mother would pimp her out for drugs. When customers stopped by the house, the mother would leave the room and the men would hold the daughter down and rape her. Because of that experience the daughter became a prostitute and endured a life of anguish and torment as she struggled to make a decent life for herself. But what kept them apart was that the mother refused to acknowledge what she had done to her daughter.

So, the daughter made it a point of hanging out at the hospice so that the mother knew she was going to die alone. Even after the mother died, the daughter would not enter the room. And once the funeral arrangements were made, the daughter disappeared.

***

In order to keep the patients as comfortable as possible, we provide them whatever they ask for as long as it's legal. The three most common requests are for cigarettes, booze, and sex.

Considering the addictive nature of cigarettes, not surprisingly, I've had cancer patients ask for them. Even people who have not smoked in decades would beg for some last puffs. Since we didn't allow smoking in our facilities, patients were escorted to an outdoor patio where they could puff away to their heart's content. If a patient was bedridden, we'd wheel them outside.

The communal nature of smoking amazed me. Sometimes I'd see several generations of a family surrounding a patient, all of them having lit up and chatting away in a manner you seldom notice with anything else.

But smoking had its hazards. One such hazard was a patient falling asleep and dropping a smoldering cigarette into the bed covers. An even bigger risk was from smokers on oxygen, which is one hundred percent pure and quite flammable.

While we stressed the danger of an open flame or a lit cigarette close to an oxygen tank, smokers decided to risk it. We're always watching to see that they didn't, but the ambulatory patients got sneaky. What happened was that they tried it once and if nothing happened, they got complacent and tried it again until we caught them or they caught fire.

For example, one patient managed to slink away and fire up a cigarette without unplugging the cannula from his nose or turning off the oxygen. He had the cigarette in his mouth and so the flame jumped from the lighter to the cannula. I had seen what he was doing and rushed toward him just as the oxygen flashed. I smacked the cannula and hose from his face and shut the valve on the oxygen tank. Fortunately, all he suffered were minor first and second degree burns to his nose. Had the flame shot up his nostrils, or into his mouth and down his throat, he would have suffered greatly.

Booze was another request. The facility was forbidden from supplying liquor so it was up to family members to sneak in the hooch. Though the facility was supposed to be alcohol-free, when relatives and friends brought in liquor, we looked the other way. When we had a patient who asked for a drink and if he had no visitors, or his family looked down on the consumption of alcohol…well, somewhat mysteriously, a bottle of the patient's favorite adult beverage managed to appear. When a bunch of people gathered together and pulled a cork, you got a party, even if the guest of honor wasn't going to be around for long.

In their final days, a lot of patients, men and women, got sexual. It's not uncommon during a sponge bath, for the men to sport an erection, which they gladly displayed. In fact, many of them were quite proud to be so aroused despite their condition. Not only that, they wanted you to give a helping hand! Or course we didn't do that. For a particularly randy patient, a whack of a pen or pencil on the offending member was enough to make it go away. Some of the men got grabby and when that happened, you had to be strict about them not touching you.

Unfortunately for Ms. Donna, one of my favorite nurses and a good friend, she finds herself the recipient of many unwanted sexual advances, either from the youngest or the oldest of our male patients. What most infuriates Ms. Donna is that she doesn't like men because of a lifetime of bad experiences with them. For some reason, she keeps getting invited into bed by our randy patients. Some try to cajole her by explaining they don't have much longer to live and would appreciate the opportunity for one more chance for sex. Others have had penile implants and want to show her how well they work.

When the women got frisky, what they did was throw off the covers and masturbate in the open. In that case, we closed the door if possible or asked them to cover up.

\*\*\*

I'm surprised by the misconceptions about what we do in hospice. These suspicions become barriers to effective symptom management. Many patients don't trust us. Sadly, one man told us that hospice was a killing place because patients arrived alive and left dead.

While family members were aggrieved to see their loved ones go, that was not always the case, which put us in an awkward situation. Family members arrived for the final visit, expecting their loved one to pass away within a day or two.

But sometimes the patients hung on or even rallied. The family members had made their peace with the death and wanted to get on with their lives. Some thought that we in hospice controlled the process and didn't believe us when we told them that we had to let nature take its course. The families got impatient and asked, "When can we go home?"

Some were on vacation time and visiting from far away, spending money on hotels and meals. They sincerely wanted to be at the patient's bedside in the final moments and resented having to stick around for an open-ended amount of time.

Often, we were asked to give the patient the "magic" shot to end their life, and the families were disappointed when we told them that those don't exist. This was a hospice, not a veterinary clinic.

Even in hospice we had to guard for suspicious deaths. Either a relative or a friend honestly wanted to see their loved one move on, or there might have been an ulterior motive at work such as revenge or keeping a patient from spilling an uncomfortable secret.

In every case, our mandate in hospice was to let our patients die with dignity. Every time one of them passed on, I would tell their survivors that they had earned their wings and flown to heaven.

# CHAPTER 19

As experienced as I now was in hospice care, both as a nurse and a supervisor, every day brought new challenges and new opportunities for me to learn.

But I also had a life outside hospice. One priority for Jamian and me was adding to our family. Though we had one beautiful daughter, we wanted more children.

Something else that prompted my desire for another child was the guilt over losing my firstborn, Alrick, 26 years ago. You never get over the loss of a child, and my mind was burdened with so many what-ifs that I could've done to save his life. When I'm alone and in a dark mood, I can still hear the thunk of his cold, lifeless body when the Jamaican medical examiner callously dropped him on the steel examination table. Nothing I can ever do will bring him back, but regardless, most everything of what I do is done in his memory.

In February 2017, I became pregnant again. During the first ultrasound, when the technician shared the news that I was carrying fraternal twins, both boys, I froze, stunned by the news. *Twins?* I had enough trouble with my one daughter, how was I going to manage two boys? But that was a good problem.

Then the closer I got to the delivery date, difficulties with my health set in. I suffered bouts of nausea, more severe than what was normal for morning sickness. Ordinary routine smells became overpowering odors that would trigger vomiting. I couldn't drive to work without having to stop along the way to puke. As a result, I began taking back roads during my commute so I wouldn't embarrass myself.

My condition worsened to the point that I had to visit the hospital every two weeks. My morning sickness wouldn't quit, in fact it lasted all day. I was constantly dehydrated, had a worrisomely elevated heart rate, and to combat the incessant vomiting, I was given anti-nausea suppositories. I was convinced my health troubles were related to my pregnancy, but how? I didn't know. What also concerned me was that treatment to better my condition might also affect my unborn babies.

In September, I experienced intense lower back pain, contractions, and bleeding, which terrified me. I alerted my obstetrician and drove myself to the emergency room. Since I'd had a miscarriage before, I was certain of another imminent miscarriage. Unfortunately, there was no sense of urgency with the staff in the emergency room. I barely got enough attention to make me feel better and sometimes, not even that. I left out of frustration, only to repeat the process when my illness practically incapacitated me.

This revolving door in-and-out of the emergency room continued through October. I became familiar with the nurse on duty though I wasn't impressed with her abilities. During this particular visit, I was in a great deal of pain and under considerable duress. Though normally I am a calm and agreeable patient, when she told me to sit and wait, I about lost my temper.

"Explain to me," I demanded, "what would you consider an emergency?"

My protests attracted the attention of the physician on duty. He ordered an immediate ultrasound, which itself took another thirty minutes to transpire. To make matters worse, the ultrasound technician brought along a student whom she had to coach through the procedure. The scan discovered the leg of one of my sons protruding through the cervix, a very dire condition.

My stay in the emergency room was becoming a horror show and I had no control of the situation. To survive, I blocked out the experience and went numb. I was in denial about my circumstances. I was used to comforting others, and here I could find no way to comfort myself.

The doctor told the staff to prepare the room for labor and delivery. I feared that the worst was about to happen and because of this remembered the exact date: October 12, 2017. He would do what he could to keep the babies in the womb and stop my contractions, but warned that the situation did not bode well for safe delivery.

Even under normal circumstances, childbirth is not a time for decorum. This time, to add to my indignity, I was positioned with my head down and my legs in the air so gravity could aid in keeping my babies inside the cervix. Because of my nausea I had not eaten for days and the only sustenance I was provided was ice chips. I was uncomfortable, famished, weak, and very scared.

The staff monitored my condition, and on October 16—after four days in constant labor—the doctor said there was little hope of saving the babies. At this point, every minute we delayed in delivering them only increased the risk of me getting a serious infection and possibly dying.

Forty-five minutes later, the child I came to call Baby A was stillborn. A few minutes later, Baby B was born. He was so small but I could feel his tiny heartbeat. I named him Dustin, which means fighter. But he had been born too premature and no matter how hard I prayed that he'd live, he didn't survive past a few minutes.

I felt so helpless at losing yet another child. During my life, this made four: Alrick, two miscarriages, and now, Dustin. What had I done to deserve such tragedy? My mind rang with recriminations that only a mother knows upon losing a child.

When I lost Alrick, I felt so much heartbreak that I wanted no memory of the pain. Because of that I destroyed every reminder that I had of him—photos, his birth certificate, any and all letters with a mention of his name.

This time though, I didn't want to forget these two babies. Since a Social Security number is now assigned at each live birth, I ordered the staff to keep every record of Dustin. I wanted to keep my babies close to me as long as possible and so they were laid side-by-side in a nearby crib. To preserve their bodies, I requested that my room's temperature be lowered until it was positively chilly.

Friends stopped by to mourn my loss. Upon entering my room, they were taken aback by the near-frigid temperature. When I explained why I had done so, they expressed surprise at seeing my babies and asked, "Why keep them in the room?" Like most Americans, they were creeped out by the proximity of the dead.

I said that they were my babies and I didn't want them tossed aside without the proper respect given to their passing. Moreover, having the babies in the room wasn't as bad as the prospect of leaving without them.

Early that evening, my two lost sons were finally taken away. Within minutes after the delivery, my body began to heal though my spirit would take a long time to recover. Shortly thereafter, I was discharged from the hospital. I left sad and broken, disoriented with grief and unable to contain what had happened.

Jamian had gone to work, and my house was a dark and lonely place. I was in such despair that I was convinced that I would be better off dead. When so much sorrow falls upon you, you think that you never want to feel better. You decide that to aspire for happiness will somehow tarnish the significance of this sorrow.

At home there was nothing to occupy me except for housework, which I hated even more than being sad. The walls closed in around me and what saved me was that not even my heartbreak could overpower my distaste at being bored. So, I returned to work.

My coworkers were well aware of my troubles, and when I walked in, they asked, "Petergay, why are you here?" They knew I was a workaholic, but returning to duty only nine short days after losing my babies astonished even them.

When I opened up about my sadness over my double miscarriage, one of the other nurses replied that she had also had a miscarriage. Another nurse admitted to four miscarriages. The administrative assistant also had a miscarriage. It turned out that half of the staff in the hospice had experienced miscarriages. While these admissions didn't diminish my regrets, knowing that I wasn't alone gave me hope. Their shared memories and empathy prompted me to get up and keep going.

***

As much as I love my career and see how it has enriched my life, I've learned that not everyone who works in hospice should work in hospice. The demands of the job can be exceptionally trying, so much so, that hospice nurses, like those who work in psychiatry, tend to be a little off. This profession attracts all kinds of characters. The public regards hospice nurses as angels but we're just people. Like anyone else, we are flawed to varying degrees and likewise have our good days and bad days.

What we have to be on guard for are those individuals who are susceptible to drug abuse. The temptations and opportunities are great. Sadly, within the last few years, the proliferation of opiates has ended many a promising career. Since nurses are entrusted with the administration of medications, they can easily pilfer drugs. Hospitals are diligent about scanning meds for inventory control, but with every solution, people soon find ways to cheat. A second tactic to get drugs is to assist the families of hospice patients, who are often elderly, and take advantage of their naivety.

Another issue is that many nurses are drama queens. They will manipulate situations to keep themselves at the center of attention. Not only does this mean that the focus of their energy is not the patient but themselves, it also means that we supervisors have to divide our vigilance between the welfare of the patient and making sure that our troublesome nurses do not cause more problems than what we already have.

When I first arrived at one supervisory position, I had a nurse openly challenge me. She was an LPN from Florida and bragged to the rest of the staff what she would and what she wouldn't do. I did my best to ignore her. In the event of a disagreement, she claimed to know other managers who would take her word over mine. But I didn't put up with her foolishness and would write her up when she failed to perform as required. She'd then report to Human Resources and cry her way back into their good graces.

But this nurse wouldn't learn. She discovered that a volunteer at our hospice was having money problems. The nurse offered to help manage the volunteer's finances if she was added to her bank account. Additionally, the nurse pressured the volunteer into amending her will to benefit the nurse. Like all drama queens, this nurse was a master manipulator and the volunteer was too intimidated to report her.

Another nurse managed to get the volunteer to share her troubles. When the truth of the drama queen was revealed, we reported her to HR and she was promptly dismissed.

Usually, drama-queen nurses are seldom as blatant as this one. Most are clever and they know how close to push their behavior without crossing a line that requires immediate disciplinary action. But a good supervisor can identify a drama queen and lay out the rules. When you articulate your expectations this way and hold people to them, you earn everyone's respect.

Even then, people try to be clever in ways that bend the rules. I had one weekend nurse who was on the phone all day and checking in with friends instead of minding her duties with the patients. Worse, if her friends were moody, she was moody. Such behavior astounded me. I had struggled so hard to become a hospice nurse, and here I saw individuals like her tossing aside what they had invested so much time and money to achieve.

In another situation, I had a husband and wife come work for me as nurses with the wife as a supervisor. However, our employment regulations didn't allow for one spouse to supervise another.

To get around that rule, they pretended that they were cousins to explain why they spent so much time around each other. However, no one was fooled and when the truth came out, they resigned from my staff rather than face disciplinary action.

\*\*\*

But my most trying stories are those concerning my patients. They range from the tragic to the humorous, from the bizarre to the perverse.

Some of my most heartbreaking stories involve patients dying of Alzheimer's. Their affliction seems ironically cruel, as their bodies are usually in good shape but it's their mind that is hopelessly damaged. Their situation makes you really question what makes a person. You can have a regular conversation with a patient and then, their mind slips and they're somewhere else. Sometimes you can see it in their eyes and you tell yourself, "They're not there."

When they lose control like this, the best remedy is to reaffirm what they're doing and then distract them.

For example, a wife and her three sons came to visit her husband, one of our patients. They were having coffee when the father suddenly slammed his cup against the table. Enraged, he demanded to know why his wife had brought her boy-toys to see him and flaunt her indiscretions. Fortunately, the wife was a sharp cookie. She told her husband that she had broken up with her young boyfriends and had brought them to say goodbye. The husband was pleased by this and settled into a peaceful conversation.

A similar experience occurred with another patient. He abruptly stood and said that he had to hurry and catch the train. Since we're taught not to argue with a patient suffering from these delusions, I distracted him by stating, "Haven't you heard? The train's been delayed five minutes. If you leave now, you'll be waiting for nothing."

The patient considered what I said, then decided it was better to wait. Within a couple of minutes, he'd forgotten all about catching the train.

***

We in hospice become experts in death. As a patient nears death, their extremities become frighteningly cool to the touch. Their skin becomes mottled, and their lips turn blue or gray. They take shallow breaths and periods of apnea can last as long as thirty seconds before resuming breathing. They lose their appetite and even if they eat, they won't swallow. It's not uncommon for a patient to have a mouthful of uneaten food. The body relaxes and the patient has a bout of incontinence. But as they haven't eaten, there's little to clean up. The brain begins to shut down. They no longer respond to pain. Then one moment the light in their eyes fades and you know they've gone.

***

In America, we have a special affinity for animals, especially dogs. I personally don't like being around dogs, or cats for that matter, because I am allergic to their hair. Another of my objections is that often dogs are not as well trained as their owners claim they are. Consequently, during visits dogs get excited by all the strange smells and pee on everything.

But families enjoy bringing dogs into the facility, and if it helps comfort the patient, we allow it. Sometimes dogs do other crazy things, like the time one jumped on the bed and began humping the patient.

Mostly though, dogs do live up to their reputations as remarkably empathetic creatures. They get very quiet and attentive and you can feel them sharing the sorrow.

***

So you don't get the wrong idea about my profession, I have to conclude this chapter with an account of another nurse, one of exemplary character, and a model professional.

This particular nurse was an exceptionally attractive blonde, always capable and poised regardless of the trials confronting her. You could be jealous of her if you weren't in in awe of her abilities and aplomb.

After a certain patient in her care had passed on, this nurse related to me that she and the patient had a similar history.

"What do you mean?" I asked.

"The patient had been addicted to crack and supported her habit with prostitution. I had done the same thing."

I couldn't believe it. This nurse seemed to have everything going for her, how was this possible?

"I had fallen as low as one could," she explained. "There wasn't anything I wouldn't do for money and drugs. Then I nearly died from an overdose."

Her face brightened unexpectedly. "But there was a blessing in what happened."

"What do you mean?"

"The experience brought me to God. It was through Him that I survived and found Jesus. Soon after that I met a loving man who became my husband, and we worked together so I could have this career."

Despite what I'd suffered, there was little in my life that could match what this nurse had endured and survived. Moreover, she didn't shy from relating her experience as a means to inspire others that no matter how hard life knocks you down, don't ever give up. I saw her as an example. If she was brave enough to share her tribulations and triumphs, so could I. It was at that point that I decided to write my story.

# CHAPTER 20

I've come to see death as a transition. Atheists are keen to point out that our existence on earth is all we have, and when we die, then that is it.

But I don't believe it. Just because we can't measure something doesn't mean it doesn't exist. How can we measure happiness? Or sadness? Or heartbreak? Only a fool would claim those emotions don't exist.

Likewise, answers to the mysteries of death, the afterlife, and the existence of a soul continue to evade us, but that does not make them any less real or relevant or, most of all, important.

While I hold traditional views on God, I have my own spiritual place that I retreat to. Though I consider myself religious I also am aware of the supernatural. You can't spend any time working in hospice and not feel the presence of souls who have departed their physical bodies. We have a name for such entities; we call them ghosts.

In the hospice where I work we've had patients, visitors, and even the medical staff see the ghosts of people that we person-ally knew and who had passed on. Many patients witness a mys-terious light floating through the halls at odd and random times. Some nurses hear whistling whose source they can't locate. If you work the night shift, all through the wee hours you will see furtive movement out the corner of your eye. Even those who claim that there are no such things as ghosts or spirits testify to the eerie and unsettling movements.

In every culture, dying and death evoke the supernatural. The dead have passed through a veil, one that we imagine can be crossed again. In hospice, we don't deny that being in this transitional place between life and death makes us aware of ghosts and strange happenings.

When patients are close to dying, they often claim to have met and spoken with others who have preceded them into the afterlife. It's not unusual for us nurses to feel the presence of a recently departed patient as if their soul had some reason to linger. Many times, both patients and staff relate seeing a child in the facility, someone who we can never verify was actually there.

The sense of the supernatural not only extends to visitations by ghosts but also to the building itself. While we fill the rooms based on vacancy, each room has definite characteristics and develops a unique reputation.

Anyone who has spent any time in Room 101 has seen a small boy. He appears dressed head to toe in white, and is animated and talkative like you'd expect from any normal boy. But about the time you ask yourself what he was doing here, he vanishes and you wonder if you weren't hallucinating. The mystery of this strange and fleeting boy gets even more bizarre. One of our nurses had brought in her three-year-old daughter, who then surprised us with her stories of not only seeing this phantom child, but engaging him in conversation.

Was it coincidence that every patient suffering from a head

injury was assigned to Room 202? It was uncanny that even when we had a new nurse who had no awareness of Room 202's reputation, she would still assign an incoming head-injury patient to that room.

Room 203 earned a different record. It was in that room where the older patients would take a long time to pass on. We had a certain elderly woman who arrived having made her peace and was ready to die. We had some maintenance issues in her first room so we had to move her to Room 203. Though she didn't appear better, she still hadn't passed on. Two days later, she demanded, "Why am I still here? I'm tired of this and am ready to die."

The first time something unusual like this happened to me was early in my nursing career when I lived in Fort Lauderdale. I was assigned to an agency to deal with patients the facility didn't want to handle. When I arrived, the CNA gave me the facility's report on the patient, a middle-aged woman confined to her bed. The patient claimed to have seen a stranger through the curtains of her room, which was suspicious because the room faced an upper-level balcony. She described the stranger as a tall man who limped with a cane. When she told me she had just seen the stranger, I opened the doors but didn't see anyone outside.

Later, the patient's daughter called from New York. She had a dream that her grandfather, the patient's father, who had died two years prior and walked with a cane, had visited her. He told her that he was going to fetch his daughter, my patient, which explained the presence of the selfsame stranger.

Other inexplicable happenings included the arrival of a canary whenever a patient was close to death. When the patient expired, then the canary disappeared. After several weeks, the canary flew away for good, only to be replaced the following year by a robin that served as the messenger of death.

But these couriers of someone's passing weren't limited to birds. For a while we had a flower in the lobby that would droop whenever a patient died, and then the next day, the flower would perk back up. And something else we all noticed, that on many occasions, when a patient was about to die, the flowers in the room emitted an unusual and overly sweet fragrance.

***

Every relative and visitor reacts differently to death. I've seen families in such denial that loved ones tried desperately to wake their dead relative. I had a patient in her forties die, and when I proceeded downstairs to tell her mother and uncle, they both fainted as if her passing was completely unexpected.

Another patient was in his sixties and dying of cancer. Incredibly, his mother, who was still alive, admonished him for not praying hard enough—hence his illness—and took away his TV. She said that he had to suffer with his pain. She even donated her car to the church, thinking that the financial sacrifice and loss of convenience would serve as penance for her son's irreligious living and thus bring God's healing.

We tend to forget that every religion has its own rituals for paying respects to the dying and the deceased. But equally, in every religion, skepticism and questions about life and death bring brittle tension in the ensuing clash between faith and religion.

Hindus provide idols for the dying to cultivate favor with their deities. After death, the survivors sing to help transport the fallen to Nirvana. But Hindus are no more enlightened than the rest of us. Similar to the Christian example I related above, a certain Hindu mother wanted her daughter to suffer and in doing so, confess for her transgressions against the family.

Even those who work in hospice are not spared the anguish. I shared my loss of Alrick with one of our attending physicians, Dr. Panchshil Patel, and he stated that he wouldn't be upset if his daughter had died.

I looked at him skeptically. "I don't believe you."

He said, "I believe in reincarnation and people die when their mission on earth is done. Your son completed his good deed, and his assignment was done."

"Even so," I replied, "I still miss him a great deal." Considering that I had challenged Dr. Patel and that I'm not Hindu, I still drew comfort from what he shared. It was remarkable that an educated and forthright man like himself had to weigh his heartache against his spiritual convictions.

Buddhists also have many rituals to send off their loved ones into the afterlife. They tend to regard death as one's release from mortal suffering and another step in their spiritual journey. I found it interesting that each sect or group within Buddhism has its own spin on their rituals. Korean Buddhists tend to dress their departed in black, where most religions enshroud their dead in white.

The one group that struggles the most with death are atheists. For many of them, they've spent a good part of their lives actively denying the existence of God and dismissing any belief in an afterlife as a reassuring delusion. Suddenly they've run smack into their own mortality and they're terrified by their forthcoming demise. With no regard for the hereafter, death means complete and absolute oblivion. Just as among the religious, death demands reconciliation between faith and religion, and so it is with atheists, only there is little to bring solace as they lack both faith and belief in a God in whatever form. They have no answers, only questions and fear of the unknown. This realization shocks them, and they grapple in vain to find a place in the universe. Most of them in hospice become restless and can't get comfortable with the fact that according to their beliefs, once they die, they are gone forever, and this ruthless finality fills them with terror.

*** 

But there's an inspiring counterpoint to what I just shared. In my career with hospice I've met many memorable individuals, and there was one patient who touched me so deeply that I dedicate this chapter to him.

His name was Richard Sparks, a person unlike any other patient that I've ever had the privilege of knowing. I feel such reverence for him that I can't remember him as Richard, but as Mr. Sparks.

Before visiting him for the first time, his previous nurse warned me that he did not appreciate when the visiting nurse spent an extended amount of time with him. She requested that I schedule a home visit and then leave as quickly as possible, so that's what I was prepared to do.

My typical nursing visit lasts approximately thirty to forty-five minutes, which includes assessment and medication reconciliation. When I finally met Mr. Sparks, I discovered that he was very straightforward and quite clear regarding his expectations from the visiting nursing staff. He was emphatic in stating that he preferred morning visits between 7:30 and 8:30, and when possible, would opt for earlier visits, the briefer the better. Furthermore, he requested a phone call if the assigned staff was unable to visit within his time preference. He emphasized that he regarded nursing care visits as a necessary but unwelcome intrusion into his life.

Despite his pronouncements, my first appointment with Mr. Sparks became a complete surprise for the both of us. It turned his opinion about the nurse staff visits completely around, as well as made me realize what a warm and welcoming human being he actually was, and not some rigid taskmaster as I was led to believe. This visit lasted over an hour and a half, because we were both astonished that we had immediately developed a patient-to-nurse connection like neither of us had ever experienced. He had the most sincere manner that one could ever imagine and was as genuine and humble as any individual could be. I discovered that he and I had a lot in common, including the fact that we had both served as caddies in our younger days.

After this initial meeting, I realized that I wanted to keep him as a patient and agreed to twice-weekly visits. This was a great example of the circumstance that, though I'm supposed to comfort the patient, he instead winds up comforting me. However, I had to adhere to his time preferences in order to keep managing his case. The challenge was that my commute through Metro Atlanta traffic lasted from an hour to an hour and forty-five minutes. Considering all the possible bottlenecks and traffic jams, I decided the only way to make sure that I made the visit on time would be to show up at least an hour early and sleep in his driveway. He resided with his daughter Cindy, and because of my plan, I usually got there between 5:45 and 6:30 AM, which allowed me to rest in my car until 7:30 AM.

Though this early arrival was not my healthcare agency's requirement, I felt my sacrifice was necessary because I had to take care of Mr. Sparks and nurture this budding relationship between us. I would eagerly await our visits as I knew he had a lot of useful life-enriching stories to share, and each would nourish my soul with his anecdotes of love and kindness.

Mr. Sparks was born in Chicago, one of seven children with five surviving siblings, the oldest of which was 91. He reminisced often about Ralph—nicknamed "Sparky"—and Don, Norman, John, and Judy. He proudly served in the U.S. Army, and he recollected his days as a soldier, including the time he hitchhiked home after getting released from active duty.

Mr. Sparks doted on his family, especially his six children who were Jeff, Betsy, Cindy, Cathy, Vickie, and Rick. His grandchildren were always mentioned in weekly updates, and as I listened to him discuss his children I tried to figure out which was his favorite. Even after all our time together, I was never able to discover his preferred, as he was clever and gracious enough to highlight each child and would take it in turn to share unique memories of every one of them.

Among his most treasured recollections was the time when he took his entire brood to Tennessee to see the snow. Once there, he towed them with ropes behind his truck so they could slide along the snow for wintertime fun. After all this effort to play in the winter weather, they returned to their Georgia home, only to plow through another snow storm. He often repeated his stories, but in each re-telling they still sounded fresh and exciting as new memories injected his stories with additional detail and vitality.

Each visit usually ended with kind and encouraging words from him. He taught me how to see the best in everything and encouraged me to enjoy spending quality time with the people who meant the most to me.

From visit to visit, I couldn't help but notice that as Mr. Sparks got weaker and weaker, he seemed more relaxed and peaceful though he was fully aware that he was transitioning toward the end of life. We often discussed his own mortality and he assured me that his only wish was for his children to remain on one accord at the time of his death, and his desire to have continued peace and unity among them.

Mr. Sparks had a lot of sentimental attachments to the state of Tennessee. He graduated from the University of Tennessee, which was where he met his wife, and they spent their honeymoon in Knoxville. He frequently talked about his favorite places to visit, and reminisced about his college days and all the fun he had while studying as an undergrad. Mr. Sparks was so dedicated to the University of Tennessee that after his last doctor's appointment, when he was informed that there was nothing else that could be done to save his life, he refused to remove his University of Tennessee shirt.

He died a few days later while wearing the same shirt. I, and my nursing assistant ironically named Miracle, spent time with him during his last moments. Throughout, he remained aware and could respond with blinking and hand grasps as he faded away. It was during this time that I noticed that Mr. Sparks would become more relaxed with the singing of one of his favorite songs, "Amazing Grace."

Miracle and I left Mr. Sparks to tend to other patients. At 4:40

PM I felt the need to call his home to see how things were going with the family. After saying hello, his daughter Cindy related, "Dad just took his last breath, thanks for calling at this time."

At his time of death, I was only seven minutes away from my next patient, a routine visit with no reported difficulties, so I returned straightaway to Mr. Sparks' home.

He died on February 10, 2017, and I can still remember that day's beautiful sunset. The memory of Mr. Sparks and his delightful family will last forever in my heart. I feel blessed to have had the opportunity to care for such an extraordinary human being, whose light brightened my days with life lessons that will linger within me forever.

*\*\**

So, what have I learned? What is it that I want to share? What is my message that I hope will enrich your life and put you on the path to being a better person?

To begin, working in hospice opened my eyes and has given me a new and appreciative perspective on life. My relationships with patients taught me a lot about myself. I've learned to pick my battles; that I can't tilt at windmills, but at the same time, occasionally I do have to stand my ground.

I've learned to maintain a positive outlook. That's not to say to be a Pollyanna about everything. You've got to remain alert and aware, otherwise events will run you over.

What helps me remain upbeat is that I maintain my faith through a positive relationship with God. I read Scripture and I like to collect uplifting affirmations, which I share with acquaintances.

Some people may regard these positive aphorisms as clichés, but I see them as guideposts to help me keep on track. Even when you dedicate yourself to remain strong and positive, life has a way of blindsiding you and grinding you down. It's easy to succumb to the notion that what you do is pointless, but you can't allow yourself to think that way.

What I've experienced in my life is a story to share, to show other people that no matter how desperate your situation may seem, there is a way forward, there is a way out. That in life, if you want to make something of yourself, you can't afford to fail and you must keep pushing forward.

Time and time again I've found myself at the crossroads. When I was younger, I lacked direction and sometimes chose the wrong way. But I learned from my mistakes and pulled myself back from the brink. It would've been too easy to succumb to bitterness and cynicism and decide that being a good person wasn't worth the effort, but instead I decided to look for the good in others and in myself. Deciding on such a path hasn't always shielded me from heartache, but with hard work and discipline, it has brought me rewards that I wouldn't have had otherwise.

I am more than a survivor. I have triumphed.

## THE END